Balanced Life
Beautiful Life

A Story of Resilience & Self-Discovery

Sirshree

Balanced Life, Beautiful Life

A Story of Resilience and Self-discovery

By **Sirshree** Tejparkhi

Copyright © Tejgyan Global Foundation

All Rights Reserved 2023

Tejgyan Global Foundation is a charitable organization with its headquarters in Pune, India.

ISBN : 978-93-90607-80-8

Published by WOW Publishings Pvt. Ltd., India

First Edition published in August 2023

Printed and bound by Trinity Academy, Pune, INDIA

Copyright and publishing rights are vested exclusively with WOW Publishings Pvt. Ltd. This book is sold subject to the condition that it shall not by way of trade or otherwise, be lent, resold, hired out, or otherwise circulated without the publisher's prior written consent in any form of binding or cover other than that in which it is published and without a similar condition including this condition being imposed on the subsequent purchaser and without limiting the rights under copyright reserved above, no part of this publication may be reproduced, stored in or introduced into a retrieval system, or transmitted, in any form, or by any means, electronic, mechanical, photocopying, recording or otherwise, without the prior written permission of both the copyright owner and the above-mentioned publisher of this book. Any person who does any unauthorized act in relation to this publication may be liable to criminal prosecution and civil claims for damages.

Although the author and publisher have made every effort to ensure accuracy of content in this book, they hereby disclaim any liability to any party for any loss, damage, or disruption caused by errors or omissions, resulting from negligence, accident, or any other cause. Readers are advised to take full responsibility to exercise discretion in understanding and applying the content of this book.

To those
who brave life's challenges,
who seek balance amid life's tempests,
who harmonize chaos and calm,
thus awakening the indomitable
spirit of resilience.

Contents

Prologue		7
1.	A Scream of Desperation	13
2.	The Glamorous Trap	16
3.	A Blast from the Past	23
4.	A Fall from Grace	26
5.	Rock Bottom	31
6.	Nowhere Left But Up	34
7.	Everyone Has Struggles	43
8.	Mending Broken Bonds	48
9.	The 3D Formula	54
10.	No Pain, No Gain	62
11.	An Opportunity Knocks	66
12.	Trapped in a Maelstrom	69
13.	Struggling Between Past and Future	73
14.	Breaking Free from Fear	80
15.	Beyond the Whys, Embracing the Hows	86
16.	Rising Above Past Missteps	90
17.	Quest for Creative Fulfillment	96
18.	Tempted by the Allure	105

19.	From Pressure to Pride	112
20.	A Birthday Call with Lingering Guilt	119
21.	Stamping Out Judgment	126
22.	Planting the Seeds of Abundance	139
23.	The Recipe for Perfect Health	150
24.	Step by Step	162
25.	Discovering the Middle Ground	167
26.	Echoes of a Restless Heart	171
27.	Beneath the Mask	175
28.	Embracing the Ever-Evolving Path	179
29.	Choosing the Path Less Comfortable	183
30.	Navigating the Waves of Non-acceptance	187
31.	Back to the Future	199
32.	The Enigma of Existence	202
33.	The Divine Play	211
	Epilogue	220
	Appendix	224-228

Prologue

A life devoid of risks may seem serene, yet true resilience is not found in avoiding adversity but in navigating life's storms with tranquility and joy.

As the clock ticked closer to the end of the workday on a Friday afternoon, anticipation filled the air among the employees. The fashion industry had always been known for its long and grueling work weeks, and everyone was looking forward to the weekend to unwind and recharge. But amidst the prevailing fatigue, Esha stood out from the rest. Her passion for her work was evident in her genuine smile that lit up her face, the unique designs she created, and the magnetic presence she exuded.

Esha made her way to the canteen for lunch, and as she entered, she spotted Anita, her junior colleague, sitting alone, lost in deep thought. Anita had joined the firm only a few months ago. Still, she had already proven to be exceptionally skilled in her work, with her creative ideas and efforts reminding Esha of her early days in the fashion industry. The two quickly formed a strong bond, with Anita often seeking Esha's guidance and looking up to her as a mentor.

"Hey, Anita! Are you having yet another out-of-the-world design racing through your mind?" Esha joked as she approached Anita, trying to lighten her mood.

"I wish that was the case. I feel like my ideas have gone on vacation or something. I've been struggling for a whole week on this new project. I can't seem to think of any new ideas. And it's not the first time I've hit a creative slump. I've been stuck in this unproductive phase for a while now, and it's driving me crazy. I even feel guilty when I see others being productive. Do you think I could get fired for going through this unproductive slump?" Anita expressed her concerns with a sigh.

Esha placed a comforting hand on Anita's shoulder, her empathy evident in her voice. "Anita, relax! No one's going to fire you, and you've got no reason to feel guilty. We all have those days when designs just don't flow easily, but don't stress too much about it! Is that why you've been feeling low lately?" Esha reassured her, her tone gentle and calm.

Anita nodded, her eyes filled with worry. "Yes, most likely. It's been stressful trying to prove myself since I'm still new here. I've heard about how hard you've worked throughout your career. I aspire to be as successful as you." Anita confided, her voice tinged with admiration.

"It's great to hear that you want to keep improving, but you don't know my entire story. I didn't get here in just a few months! It took numerous projects, challenging experiences, major mistakes, and invaluable life lessons for me to reach where I am. You will get there too, and even go beyond. Just be patient; if you ever need help, feel free to come to me. You know I'm always ready to lend you a hand," Esha reassured Anita with a warm smile before returning to her desk.

Anita's mind swirled with thoughts as she reflected on Esha's words. It made sense, she thought. She needed to have patience and keep moving forward. However, there was still that persistent fear that if she paused to catch her breath, life would seize the opportunity to drag her down, unleashing a torrent of obstacles in her path. Lost in her usual quicksand of worries, Anita suddenly recalled Esha mentioning that she, too, had faced tough times in her life. Yet, today, she has risen to become a passionate designer, firmly established among the higher ranks of the profession.

With renewed determination, Anita decided to reach out to Esha for further guidance. She needed someone to help her break free from her cycle of unproductivity. Esha warmly agreed to meet at her house the next day, where they could have a peaceful conversation and take their time to discuss Anita's concerns in depth. As Anita left the canteen, she felt a glimmer of hope and a sense of gratitude for having someone like Esha in her corner. Little did she know that this meeting would be a turning point in her career, setting her on a path to success in the challenging yet rewarding world of fashion.

Anita stood in awe as she gazed at Esha's enchanting house. The sunlight streamed through the large windows, casting a warm glow on the cozy interior. The walls were adorned with small polaroids capturing precious moments of Esha's life, from family gatherings to fun outings with friends and her roommate. At the center of this collage was a lit frame showcasing a dark silhouette of the Buddha in a meditative posture with light radiating all around it. Mini bookshelves lined the walls, filled with an eclectic collection of books on various topics, reflecting Esha's diverse interests. The ceiling was adorned with unique lights, carefully arranged in an artistic manner, adding a touch of whimsy to the space. The atmosphere was serene, exuding a sense of peace and tranquility.

Anita felt instantly at ease as she sat on the fuzzy carpet by the wall, adorned with colorful cushions. The carpet felt soft and comforting beneath her, and she couldn't help but notice the attention to detail in Esha's home. The room was tastefully decorated, reflecting Esha's impeccable sense of style.

"I love your house! It's so peaceful and calm, yet it's filled with such lavish beauty," Anita said, taking in the surroundings with admiration.

Esha smiled, her eyes lighting up with pride. "Thank you! I've put a lot of thought and effort into creating a space that reflects my personality and brings me joy."

Anita nodded, feeling a pang of envy as she compared Esha's well-organized and inviting home to her own cluttered and chaotic living space. She couldn't help but feel a twinge of longing for the peace and order that seemed to permeate Esha's house.

"I feel quite the opposite, though," Anita continued, her voice tinged with frustration. "I've been a mess lately, and the storm in my mind is filled with fear of failure. I'm stressed and worried about how to cope with all the challenges. It's not just my designs; I feel like I've lost control of life in general."

Esha's expression softened with empathy as she reached out and placed a comforting hand on Anita's shoulder. "Anita, it's okay to feel overwhelmed sometimes. We all go through rough patches in life. But remember, it's just a passing phase. It's an opportunity to learn, grow, and become even stronger and more resilient."

Anita nodded, her eyes filled with gratitude. Esha's words resonated with her; she found comfort in her friend's reassurance. She took a deep breath, feeling a glimmer of hope amidst the storm of her thoughts.

"Esha, I know this might be personal, and I'm sorry if I'm crossing any boundaries," Anita began hesitantly. "But can you tell me what happened to you a few years ago? They say you went through a tough time, too, right? How did you turn things around? It would really help me if you could share."

Esha's kind demeanor put Anita at ease, and she listened attentively as Esha began to share her story. Esha's words were eloquent and heartfelt, painting a vivid picture of her journey through challenges and setbacks and how she found the strength to overcome them. Anita was captivated by Esha's story, finding inspiration in her resilience and determination.

Esha's comforting smile dispelled all of Anita's concerns. "You don't have to feel awkward," Esha reassured her. "I'm not ashamed of my past. Yes, I made mistakes, but I'm proud of how I've overcome them. At one point in my life, nothing seemed worthwhile, not even life itself. But my story isn't about despair; it's about resilience. The past three years have been quite a journey, and I'd be happy to share it with you if it can be of help. So let me begin from the start - my childhood."

Amidst the warmth of a sunny Saturday afternoon, time seemed to stop as Esha shared her experiences with Anita.

I was born in Bhoojpur village on the outskirts of Chandauli near Varanasi in Uttar Pradesh. I grew up in a loving, modest household with my parents and my younger sister, Ayushi. My childhood was filled with laughter and joy, and my favorite pastimes were playing with friends, gazing at the stars in the night sky, and designing clothes for my dolls. Fashion and stargazing were my twin passions, and I had an innate love for colors and an eye for fabrics.

Even in my small village, I found inspiration in movies and fashion magazines and began designing my dresses. As time passed, my skills improved, and I even started making outfits for my friends and family. Despite the monotony of life in the small village, I had dreams that stretched far beyond the confines of Bhoojpur.

With a heart full of ambition, I moved to Delhi after completing my schooling to pursue a course in Fashion Design. It was a bold step, but I was determined to follow my dreams. I had poured my heart and soul into my studies, and after finishing my course, I set my sights on Mumbai, my dream city, for my internship. I was ready to take on the fashion world and make my mark.

As time passed, I worked tirelessly and dedicated myself to my craft. I went from small assignments to big projects with renowned fashion houses, learning the intricacies of fashion and glamor. The industry was tough and competitive, but my passion and perseverance paid off. My career flourished, and I achieved success beyond my expectations.

But then, my life took an unexpected turn. Over time, I faced challenges and setbacks that shook me to my core. I found myself struggling, feeling lost and unworthy despite my achievements. The once-glowing embers of my passion dimmed, and I found myself teetering on the edge of despair, even considering ending my life.

Esha paused momentarily, and her eyes seemed lost in the dark clouds of her past before she continued.

1

A Scream of Desperation

As I looked down from the rooftop railing I was teetering on, I could see the traffic crawling by as usual, people going about their daily mundane tasks. Everything looked minuscule and insignificant from up there. Fear gripped me as I could see my end. My feet trembled, sweat was pouring down my back, and thoughts were racing through my head. Jump, Esha. No, come on, there's nowhere else to go. No, it's too scary. GO! No, what about Ma and Dad? All their hard work? And Ayushi... what example would I be setting for her? Just go... NO.

I imagined my body hurtling down, freely falling for a while, and then Bang! Everything would be over in a pool of blood. I stepped back; Damn, I don't even have the guts to jump! A stray thought of respect filled me up for all those who managed to do this. I slid down to the floor and sat hugging my knees, tears streaming down my cheeks.

I kept lamenting: "Oh God, why me? Is everything that I've achieved finally coming to this? How would Ma and Dad have felt if I had taken this step? They have worked hard to support me and my dreams all their life. Ayushi and my friends, would they even miss me? Is there a way to get out of all this? How did I lose myself? How can I forgive myself for getting here?" All I could do was pray, "Please, God… please, get me out of this. I can't handle this anymore. Where do I go?"

As the weight of my harsh thoughts bore down on me, it felt like my head would burst from the pressure. I cursed myself, consumed by overwhelming despair and darkness. I had just lost my third job in nine months, and my financial situation was bleak. Credit debts were mounting, and job offers were nowhere to be found. Fear gnawed at me as I grappled with the gloomy reality of my circumstances.

Having witnessed others being let go from their jobs, I had often wondered how I would fare in such a situation. What would my reaction be? How would it feel? Now I knew all too well. Frustration gnawed at me, hopelessness enveloped me, and fear clenched my heart. I felt like a failure, overwhelmed by the weight of these emotions.

I swallowed the lump in my throat, my gaze turning to the stars. Tears streamed down my cheeks, and I struggled to wipe them away, blinking to clear my vision. The moon appeared to have a reddish tint, mirroring the turmoil in my mind. I was overcome with fear, feeling my emotions inextricably tied to the celestial scene above.

How could life be so cruel?

Only a couple of years back, life had been just perfect. Then, one after another, the pillars of every part of my existence began to crumble. I sought answers and found none, only sadness and loneliness.

I scanned the sky for a ray of hope but saw none. I called into the darkness for help. No one heard me. The truth of the situation hit me. I deserved everything that was coming to me. Friends and colleagues were ignoring or belittling me. I felt hopeless. There seemed to be no other option left for me than putting an end to all of this, but now even that seemed something beyond me.

Failure seemed to be my destiny, and with every decision I'd made, it was as if I'd been guided toward this abyss of misery. I couldn't hold back my tears as I wallowed in the depths of despair, questioning how everything had led to this point. The pain was overwhelming, and I spent the entire night in anguish.

I was left with no choice but to acknowledge my wrongdoings and accept the need for change. The weight of my defeat was crushing, smothering my very soul with a sense of suffocating hopelessness. As I contemplated the daunting prospect of tomorrow, I was seized by an overwhelming uncertainty that threatened to consume me entirely. The future seemed bleak and uncertain, and I felt utterly lost in the grip of my emotions.

With shaking hands, I dialed a number and collapsed onto the ground, unable to hold back my sobs. The weight of my problems felt unbearable, suffocating me. I just sobbed uncontrollably, unable to get a single word out. I cried myself to sleep, clutching the phone tightly, hoping that somehow, someway, things would get better.

2

The Glamorous Trap

I clearly remember the day almost eight years earlier when I had arrived in Mumbai, the city of my dreams. It was a bustling metropolis, overcrowded, dusty, and sweaty. I had rented a small apartment in the western suburb of Goregaon, which I shared with three other girls - Shubhra, Geeta, and Radhika.

Shubhra was an office assistant in a software firm, while Geeta and Radhika worked in a call center. Despite our different schedules, we formed a good team and split the household chores among us. The apartment was small compared to what I was used to back home, but I didn't complain. The company of my roommates made everything bearable.

"Esha, is there a water supply throughout the day? How are you going to cook? You can't keep eating outside," Ma's voice echoed through the phone as she had called for the fourth time today, worried about me living alone in the big city.

"C'mon, Ma! Stop worrying! I can cook for myself. I am a grown-up now, and I can take care of myself. It's already late at night. Please stop worrying and go to sleep," I had assured her, trying to calm her down. I then carried on, arranging my things in my new home, away from home.

Life in the big city was a rush! The daily commute from my apartment to work on the crowded Mumbai local trains took a toll on my time and energy. By the end of the day, I would be exhausted and ready to collapse on my bed. My first year in Mumbai was full of struggles, trying to adapt to the fast-paced lifestyle and the challenges of living in a big city.

Geeta and Radhika had erratic schedules, so Sundays were the only time we could meet each other. On the other hand, Shubhra and I had similar schedules, and we soon became good friends. She showed me around the city, took me to wholesale markets for shopping, and we even splurged on movies and street food stalls. It was fun, but at times I also felt nostalgic and longed for the comfort of my home in Bhoojpur.

Whenever the memories of my parents and my sister Ayushi made me feel homesick, I would find solace on the rooftop of my building. I loved stargazing. Back in Bhoojpur, my house had a big courtyard, and sitting there and watching the starlit sky was my favorite pastime. The stars in Mumbai seemed hazy and sparse due to air pollution, but it still brought me a sense of peace. As I watched the moon and stars, feeling the cool breeze on my face, I longed for the familiar comforts of home.

My first job in Mumbai was with Orchids, a well-known fashion house, where I worked as a trainee in the Production department. The office was housed in a massive twenty-two-storeyed building, and I worked on the first floor, assisting Mr. Niranjan Das, the assistant designer. Our team had three more trainees. We all worked under Niranjan's guidance. It was a challenging but exciting experience as I learned the ropes of the fashion industry in Mumbai, the city that never sleeps.

I relished my work; it was a fierce battle at first, but the camaraderie of my colleagues and mentors made it a joy. It wasn't just about gaining experience but also the chance to delve into novel designs. I even spent my free time attending shows by top designers, taking notes on their seasonal collections.

The world I found myself in was one of glitz, glamor, and ruthless competition, and yet, I couldn't have been happier. I pored over the latest trends, color schemes, and the fusion of contemporary and traditional styles. Nights and weekends were a blur of hard work and excitement, with fittings and model runs all consuming my days. Starting as a trainee, I quickly rose through the ranks.

"Congratulations, Esha! You've officially been confirmed on the rolls of Orchids as a full-time employee. You've successfully completed your training. We're delighted with your work and promoting you to Junior Designer." Ravi Ahuja, the Head of Design, welcomed me with open arms. It was my first big success, and I was filled with pride and joy.

I soon moved on to my second job, where I was the Assistant Designer. My finesse had grown as time passed, and I was now specializing in formal and Indo-Western wear. My parents, friends, and colleagues were thrilled with my creativity and dedication, but my satisfaction mattered the most. Offers from other fashion houses were pouring in, and I was later promoted to Senior Designer at Sensations, one of the top fashion houses. With my expertise in formal wear, I independently secured high-profile fashion projects and became one of the top-rated designers in my category. My designs made their way into high-end boutiques and runway shows. Seeing models donning my designs filled me with pride, and success was now firmly within my grasp. I was also being compensated handsomely for my hard work.

As I settled into my new abode in the posh locale of Cuffe Parade in South Mumbai, I felt a sense of liberation. Accompanied by my talented assistant designer and new roommate, Reema, I indulged in all the luxuries that were once out of reach. A sleek Volkswagen sedan was mine to drive, and I relished the freedom it brought.

Finally, my family had the chance to witness my success first-hand. I proudly showed them around the vibrant streets of Mumbai, treating them to delectable meals and unforgettable experiences. Ayushi's excitement was palpable, and my parents' pride in my achievements was a joy to behold. Not only had I managed to pay off my educational loans, but I could also support my family financially - a feat that filled me with immense satisfaction.

As I delved deeper into the fashion world, I discovered another facet of this industry - celebration. After the success of one of my designs, my colleagues insisted on marking the occasion with a night of revelry. I was eager to try new things and indulge in the glitz and glamor that surrounded me, so we made our way to Tryst, one of the most renowned pubs in South Mumbai.

"Hey, Esha, cheers!" Sejal handed me a glass of champagne. "This is to your success." Everyone raised their glasses, waiting for me to get a sip.

Come on, now; you don't want to seem like the odd person out... I had never tasted alcohol before in my life. My parents would have been livid if they'd seen me like this, but looking around at everyone's expectant faces, I braced myself for its first taste. As I took the first sip of the sour spirit, I felt like spitting it out. Looking at my reaction and guessing it was my first time, everyone laughed.

Ananya said, "It's okay honey, it's your first time, no worries, you'll get used to it, we did too. Why don't you try some sweet red wine instead?"

"I think I have had enough, Ananya."

"Hey, come on, the party has just begun. Don't be a spoilsport," Sakshi cut in.

"Yeah, Esha, come on, just one more drink," Sejal said, pouring me another glass.

"I don't think I can handle it," I said, hesitating.

"Don't be such a party pooper," Sejal said, smiling.

"Yeah, come on, you're one of us now," Ananya said.

The pressure was mounting, and I didn't want to be seen as a killjoy. I reluctantly took the glass and had a sip. The sweet taste made it easier to swallow, and soon I started taking bigger gulps.

As I downed the glass in one go, I felt sober one second, and the next, I felt completely out of it. I liked it, although not much later, I was in the restroom, throwing up. Sejal managed to drop me home.

She left me on the sofa and said, "Don't worry, Esha! I have a good remedy for hangovers; I'll text it to you. You'll be fine! Take care, goodnight!"

I found myself alone in the apartment as Reema had gone to visit her parents. It was the first time I felt an overwhelming sense of loneliness since I moved out. My mind started to wander, and I couldn't help but think about what my family would say if they saw me in this inebriated state. I knew they would be disappointed, but at the same time, I was giddy with excitement about exploring new experiences and pushing myself beyond my comfort zone. After all, drinking was just a part of the corporate culture, a way for people to let off steam and bond with their colleagues.

After another round of throwing up, I solemnly promised myself that I wouldn't indulge in alcohol again. However, a sense of unease lingered in my mind. Would rejecting my colleagues' invitations to socialize create a rift in our working relationship? What if it was a corporate event? Was trying new things and attending parties essential for building relationships and advancing in my career?

As time passed, attending parties became less of a social obligation and more of a routine. I couldn't explain why I kept doing it, but maybe it was the only excitement left in my days and the only way to fill the lonely hole in my heart. Each time, I hoped for something new, something exciting, but it was always the same. The loud music, the dim lights, the clinking glasses, and the fake smiles. It was exhausting, but I couldn't stop. It was as if I was addicted to the rush of being around people and the temporary escape from my guilt about my actions.

As time passed, I found myself spiraling down a dangerous path. What started as a harmless indulgence in social drinking had escalated into a full-blown addiction to hard liquor. I was completely unaware of the monster I had created within myself until it was too late. My constant partying and late nights had taken a toll on my job and health.

Despite my promises to myself to stop, I found myself trapped in a vicious cycle. The excitement of the parties and the thrill of alcohol had become more alluring than my work. I had lost sight of my dreams and the person I had once been.

But that wasn't the only habit I had picked up. I started eating at odd hours, indulging in fast food and spicy dishes. My laziness in cooking and my busy schedule led to the habit of ordering meals on a daily basis. My health started to suffer as I gained weight and became less agile. My once-svelte figure was now a distant memory, and my skin looked dull and pallid.

To make matters worse, my clashes with colleagues had increased. My success had only fueled my arrogance, and I was blind to the effect it was having on my relationships. Looking back, I can see the mistakes I made, but at that time, I was lost in my addiction, the only thing that brought excitement to my days.

As the addiction took hold of me, I began to feel more and more guilty for my actions. I knew what I was doing was wrong, but I couldn't seem to control my impulses. I would get easily agitated and emotional, lashing out at others for no reason. My colleagues started avoiding me, and even my friends from back home noticed a change in me.

I would wake up feeling sick and regretful in the morning, promising myself to quit drinking and turn my life around. But as soon as the sun went down, the cravings would return stronger than ever. I couldn't resist the temptation and would find myself back at the bar, drowning my sorrows in alcohol.

The guilt started to eat away at me, and I became more and more isolated from those around me. I knew I was hurting myself and those who cared about me, but I felt powerless to stop.

My emotions became more intense, and I found myself crying for no apparent reason or getting angry over the smallest things. I was a mess, both physically and emotionally. But even though I knew I needed help, I couldn't bring myself to ask for it. The addiction had taken over, and I was lost in my own downward spiral.

3

A Blast from the Past

As I was returning from yet another dismal meeting in the afternoon, I saw a beautiful lady waving out in my direction from the other side of the street. I looked around but didn't see anyone else. She started walking towards me, waving her hand excitedly. She came closer, "Hi! Don't you remember me?"

Observing the perplexity on my face, she spoke again, "Hey Eshu, didn't you recognize me? I'm Nandini! Have you forgotten me?"

I looked at her, wide-eyed with surprise, "Oh, Nandu… What a change! I just can't believe this. How did you manage to change so much?" I asked as I sized her up.

"Oh… that's a long story. I'll tell you everything. How have you been? It's been quite a few years since you moved to Mumbai. Sorry for being out of touch, but my flimsy excuse is that life has been hectic. Now you seem to have put on a few pounds, Eshu. I almost didn't recognize you."

I grimaced, "Well, life has been busy for me too, Nandu. I have a demanding job and a lot of responsibilities."

We walked to Dream Bean Café, just across the road. It was a cozy warm place with the aroma of freshly brewed coffee. Soft instrumental music was playing in the background. Nandini and I settled into the two corner seats overlooking the street.

As we began chatting, we started recalling and laughing over old memories and anecdotes of schoolmates and teachers. But I couldn't help but feel annoyed and jealous as Nandini told me about her successful career and happy family life.

"So Nandu, what are you doing here in Mumbai? When did you move in?"

"Last year. Anand, my husband, has his office here. We had to shift from Delhi for better business opportunities. I had invited you to my wedding, but you didn't come." Nandini gave me a hurt look.

I was filled with guilt. I remembered Ma calling me up and telling me about Nandini's wedding. But it was a phase in my career where all I could think of was to grow professionally. In the process, I lost many friendships.

I listened to Nandu as she filled me in with her details. She showed me pictures of her three-year-old daughter, Khushi. She was a close replica of Nandini - fair with big brown eyes. Nandini had started as an apprentice at a textile unit in Jaipur a)nd moved on to more extensive assignments as her career progressed. After marriage, she set up her own small-scale unit in Agra, which she coordinated from her home office here. She was an entrepreneur in her own right.

I was happy for Nandini, seeing her balancing everything - home and career - but also felt pangs of envy. I was not yet ready to share my story with her. After a long time, I felt I could connect with someone without the fear of being slighted. So, I wanted to hang on to that reassuring feeling for a while longer. However, the thought of holding back the truth made me restless. When it was time to leave, I felt I was deceiving Nandini by holding back.

"What's up with you, Eshu? I've been doing all the talking; you're just keeping silent. What is it, Eshu? I can sense your restlessness. Do you want to share something?" When I was reminded of my miserable life, I felt myself losing control of my anger.

I tried to brush off the topic, "No, no, there isn't much to talk about, Nandu. I'm just feeling a little tired." I gulped my coffee quickly and stood up to leave, trying not to let my envy and bitterness show.

"Are you sure you're okay, Eshu?" Nandini asked, concern etched on her face.

I forced a smile, "I'm fine. It was nice seeing you after so long."

I left the Café in a hurry, trying my best to hide the emotions that were threatening to spill over. As I walked out onto the street, I felt a sudden urge to escape. Without thinking twice, I hailed a cab and headed to the nearest bar.

The dimly lit bar was filled with people, and the sound of chatter and clinking glasses filled the air. I took a seat at the bar and ordered a drink. As the bartender poured me a glass of whiskey, I couldn't help but think about Nandini's success. She had a loving husband, a beautiful daughter, and a successful career. Meanwhile, I was struggling to control my own body and relationships.

The whiskey burned as it went down my throat, and I ordered another one. With each sip, my jealousy and inferiority complex seemed to grow stronger. I knew it wasn't healthy to drown my sorrows in alcohol, but I couldn't stop myself.

As the night wore on, I became more and more drunk. My thoughts were jumbled. All I knew was that I felt lost and alone. Eventually, I stumbled out of the bar and made my way back to my apartment.

4

A Fall from Grace

One day after a night of partying, I stumbled into work late. Even the bright sun seemed to glare at me, taunting me for my tardiness. My head throbbed from the previous night's excesses, and I struggled to focus on the scowl of the Chief Designer. His words were sharp, cutting through me like knives.

"Esha, how can you come in at this time?" he demanded, his tone laced with frustration. "We started at 9 a.m. It's almost lunchtime now."

Reema stood beside him, her arms folded across her chest, her expression equally unimpressed. "I sent you the designs two days ago," she said coolly, "and you haven't bothered to reply or even show up at work since then. We had to finalize the designs in your absence, and now we've lost the project because of your irresponsible behavior."

I could feel my pride swelling inside me, refusing to admit any fault. "And you didn't think to tell me any of this?" I snapped back, my words biting.

"When would I tell you?" Reema fired back, her voice rising. "You haven't been here for two days! You come home in the early hours of the morning, sleep until noon, and don't bother to answer my calls or reply to my messages. Where have you been, Esha? What's going on with you? Can't you just talk to me?"

I could feel my emotions boiling over, and I couldn't seem to control them. "Stop preaching to me!" I yelled, my voice echoing through the office. "Your lectures are so boring. That's why I don't answer your calls. And listen, I don't need your help. I can handle this on my own."

Reema looked hurt and surprised. "Esha, I'm only trying to help. I care about you."

"Well, I don't need your help," I repeated. "I don't need anyone's help."

The tension in the room was palpable, and I could feel the weight of Reema's disappointment crushing me. But at that moment, I couldn't bring myself to admit any fault, to take responsibility for my actions.

It wasn't until later, as the haze of my hangover began to lift that I realized the full extent of my mistake. I had let my pride get in the way of a true friendship, and now I had lost the project - and possibly Reema's friendship forever.

Finding no pleasure or satisfaction in the job anymore, I sought happiness elsewhere. Indulging in spicy food, hanging out late at night with my so-called friends, and turning to alcohol and smoking became habitual. As a result, my dedication and sincerity toward work dwindled.

Every facet of my life had become shaky and unstable. I was squandering away my hard-earned money on random expenses. After exhausting my credit limits, I ran out of money and had to borrow from friends, only to splurge on parties. How insensitive one can become when one indulges in such extremes!

Memories of that miserable night still give me goosebumps. I had come to the solitary shelter of the roof in a fit of desperation to find answers to some questions. The glamorous life of a fashion designer had lost its charm for me. The way my life had shaped up during the past four years had gone beyond my endurance. The roof was the only place I could think of unwinding without anyone bothering me.

Being caught up in the doldrums, I hadn't been to the roof for a few months until that night. I clearly remember my meeting with our Chief Designer, which was the beginning of my downhill journey. I had failed to deliver for the third time in the last couple of months, but we had lost a valued client this time. I was ashamed and filled with guilt.

I was at a loss for words as Mr. Desai delivered the news to me. "Sorry, Esha, but we have to let you go," he said, looking at me sternly.

"What's wrong, sir? Why?" I asked, confused and desperate to know what had happened.

"I am sure you know why. We have lost the Elegance project due to you; they have been our esteemed client for a long time, but now they have refused to renew our contract. Your performance has been dismal; your tardiness has crossed the limits; you don't keep anyone updated. I had been ignoring all that due to your talent and past track record. You were a valued asset to our team. But this time, you've gone overboard," Mr. Desai said, his voice rising with each word.

I felt a sinking feeling in my chest as he continued. "Sir, please give me a chance!" I pleaded, hoping for a miracle.

"That's what you said the last time too. You don't get along with your team members; I have been getting complaints about that too, but I was hoping you would come around. You have become overbearing, rude, and arrogant."

His words cut deep into my heart, and I struggled to hold back my tears. "Please, Sir! This will destroy my career! News spreads fast in our industry circles. Where will I go?" I begged.

"You should have heeded my warning. I have been cautioning you since your performance slackened," he replied firmly.

"Last week was the limit, Esha!" Mr. Desai bellowed, his face turning red with anger. "We had to finalize those designs with Reema's help, and what happened? They got rejected, and you're nowhere to be found! You call this work ethics?" He glared at me, his words stinging like a slap to my face. "You didn't even inform us about your leave; your phone was off! I'm sorry, but the management has no option but to let you go."

I couldn't believe what I was hearing. How could everything fall apart so quickly? I had always been a hard worker and had tried my best to get along with my team members. But it seemed like it wasn't enough.

As I walked out of Mr. Desai's office, I felt lost and hopeless; my heart felt heavy with shame and disappointment. I knew I had let down my team and myself. I had always prided myself on my work ethic and dedication, but lately, I had lost sight of what was truly important.

As the news of my firing spread throughout the office, I could feel the pitying glances and whispers of my colleagues and friends. I tried to ignore them, but it was hard not to feel like a failure. I had always been a hard worker, but lately, I had let my personal life take over, which had cost me dearly.

As soon as I reached my apartment, I slogged my way to my bed and collapsed. All the emotions I had suppressed finally erupted, and I cried my heart out. After what seemed like an eternity, I heard the front door opening. Reema was back. My heart sank at the thought of facing her. Our last conversation had ended on a bitter note, and there was an unspoken tension between us ever since.

To my relief, Reema didn't come to my room. She must have sensed that I needed space. I was grateful for that. Exhausted from all the crying, I fell into a deep slumber, oblivious to the world around me.

The next day, I woke up late. The previous day's events felt like a bad dream, but the reality hit me hard as soon as I opened my eyes. I had lost my job, my livelihood, my reputation, and the future I had imagined for myself. I felt lost and alone.

5

Rock Bottom

As messages and sympathies poured in from friends and colleagues, I couldn't bear to face anyone. I sought refuge in a bottle of vodka, left over from my last party, which helped me numb my pain. Reema returned from work and gave me a disapproving look, noticing my glass, but I ignored her. The drinking drove me even further into a dark hole, and soon I was spiraling out of control.

It was the beginning of my downfall. I registered with placement agencies and managed to secure another job, but my arrogance cost me that too. My reputation began to precede me, making it even harder to find any new opportunities. I scraped by with freelancing and small gigs recommended by my friends, but it was barely enough to sustain my lavish lifestyle. Eventually, the interest on my debts started to pile up, and I had no choice but to let my car go.

Although I tried to curb my extravagant ways, my friends' constant invitations to parties lured me in, even though my funds ran dry. After nine long months, job insecurity and the stagnation of my skills weighed heavily on my mind, and I began to lose hope.

The weight of my shame and guilt was suffocating, crushing me under its heavy burden. Every time I thought of asking Dad for money, I felt a deep-seated sense of embarrassment. It wasn't long ago that I supported my parents, but now I had become a burden on them, and the guilt consumed me.

Back in Bhoojpur, my parents were growing increasingly worried about me. They pleaded with me to return home, hoping to pull me out of the hedonistic lifestyle that had taken hold of me. But I couldn't bear the thought of giving up my reckless ways, and the helplessness that came with it was overwhelming. Despite their attempts to get me to seek counseling, my rapid descent made it difficult for me to listen to them.

As time passed, my situation only grew worse. Friends and colleagues avoided me or called only to collect on debts, and my ex-colleagues stopped responding to my messages altogether. My erratic behavior and mood swings had driven everyone away. I had so-called friends, but I could rely on none, and the loneliness only added to my despair.

Depression had set in, and I was losing the battle against my negative thoughts. My once-healthy confidence had all but depleted, leaving me hopeless and helpless. Self-doubt consumed me, and thoughts of facing people filled me with anxiety. My condition worsened with each passing day, and the guilt and helplessness grew stronger.

The question loomed over me: Even if I did turn my life around, would my family, friends, and colleagues ever accept me again? It was a terrifying thought, but one that I couldn't escape. The shame and guilt were a constant weight on my shoulders, and I didn't know how to break free from the vicious cycle of escapism and self-destruction that had taken hold of me.

The weight of existence had become too much to bear, and I longed for nothing more than to escape the pain and misery that plagued me at every turn. With each passing day, the world felt like an increasingly hostile and unforgiving place, and the people in it seemed to take pleasure in my suffering.

That is how I found myself teetering on the rooftop's edge, my heart heavy with despair. The abyss that yawned before me was both terrifying and alluring, promising release from the torment of my existence.

6

Nowhere Left But Up

The next morning was excruciating. My head throbbed with every movement, and my body felt like lead as I dragged myself out of bed. I had barely slept, tossing and turning all night, consumed by thoughts of the previous night's events. The memory of my failed suicide attempt was still fresh in my mind, and I couldn't shake the feeling of utter despair.

As I dressed, I tried my best to appear presentable, but my reflection in the mirror told a different story. My eyes were swollen from tears, and my face was blotchy and red. Reema had already left for work, leaving me alone with my thoughts and regrets.

Meeting Nandini felt like my only hope, my last chance at redemption. She had been worried sick after my desperate phone call the previous night, and I couldn't bear the thought of disappointing her. When I arrived at her house, I was struck by its simple elegance, a far cry from the cluttered mess at my apartment.

As we sat down to talk, Nandini's warm smile and comforting words put me at ease. She offered me, Kachori, my favorite snack, a small but meaningful gesture that made me feel seen and understood. But despite her kindness, I couldn't shake the nagging feeling of inadequacy. What if she judged me for my mistakes? What if she couldn't forgive me for the pain I had caused?

Nandini must have sensed my hesitation because she spoke up, her voice gentle but firm. "Perhaps talking about it would make you feel better? I completely understand if you just need someone to be there." Her words were like a lifeline, and I clung to them desperately, afraid to let go.

I took a deep breath and began to speak, my words stumbling out in a jumble of sobs and half-formed thoughts. But as I spoke, something shifted inside me. The weight of my guilt and shame felt a little lighter, and the darkness that had consumed me slowly began to recede. Nandini listened with compassion and understanding, without judging or criticizing.

As we talked, I realized I didn't have to face my problems alone. Some people genuinely cared about me and were willing to stand by me, even during my darkest moments. For the first time in a long while, I felt a glimmer of hope that maybe, just maybe, things could get better.

As I finished recounting my story, tears streamed down my face, and Nandu hugged me tightly, her eyes brimming with tears. I felt a weight lifted off my shoulders; I had finally shared my burden with someone. Throughout my entire narration, Nandini listened intently without interrupting, and her empathetic presence gave me the space to vent out the painful emotions I had buried deep inside.

Feeling pitiful, I said, "Nandu, I really need to get out of this quicksand. I was foolishly lured into this extreme lifestyle for pleasure, and now I'm paying the price. I need to get out of it."

Nandu spoke in a measured, soothing tone. "Eshu, we'll get you out of this situation. Don't worry; we'll do it together."

I let out a sigh. "But I've ruined my life. My friends and family have given up on me, and I don't dare to face them anymore. I've lost my reputation, and I'm out of work. Some people tried to help me in the beginning, but they failed. How can you help me?"

Nandu paused and then spoke with conviction. "Esha, you can regain everything and attain a balanced and beautiful life. I know you want to get out of this situation, but first, you must choose between solving this, moving on, and becoming a winner, or staying in this state, despairing over it, and doing nothing. I promise I'll be with you and ready to help whenever you feel ready to move towards rebuilding the balance in your life." She laid her hand on mine.

Her words brought tears to my eyes again. The thought that someone wanted to help and care for me was enough to fill me with elation. "I really want a better life, Nandu. I want to overcome all this. I'm willing to do everything it takes."

Nandu replied with a smile, "That's great, Eshu! And I promise you'll be much better. It takes courage to make this choice. Just have patience, and we'll succeed." Her words made me feel better. At that moment, I didn't know whether it was more of a pep talk or would really work. But the idea that she was prepared to help me and that I was at least ready to try was a huge relief. Somehow, it made me feel less guilty, less restless, and less hopeless.

Nandu continued, "When faced with a situation like yours, many people wonder whether they should continue what they're doing or quit. In other words, they try to find an escape, a way to free themselves from their situations, hoping that they will be rid of their burden.

"To escape, some may even try to put an end to their lives. I'm not saying they're cowards; it takes courage even to make that decision. But if a person has so much courage, why not choose to live, bounce back, and overcome the challenges? What seems like courage to end one's life turns out to be driven by the fear of facing what life throws at us. Why not give yourself another chance, another way?"

"Are you reading my mind, Nandu? I've been feeling so depressed and low lately that I really feel I've had enough of this life. This job was my passion. It was my dream that brought me here and built this career. I was doing so well, but then I ruined everything. Now…"

"Okay, wait! Always remind yourself to seek solutions, not problems, or you'll be stuck forever. Let's focus on how we can make things better… right?" Nandini interrupted with an encouraging smile.

I nodded, feeling grateful for her presence and guidance. "You're right, Nandu. I need to focus on the solutions instead of wallowing in my problems. But it's hard to see a way out right now."

"I understand, Eshu. But there's always a way out, even if it's not immediately clear. Let's start by taking things one step at a time. When you find yourself at rock bottom, the only place left to go is up."

Then Nandu shared her "little success mantra" with me. "To begin, you need to accept everything that has happened. This will help you overcome unhappiness or any other negative feelings since acknowledging them is always the first step. You may call it a mantra. I call it the 'little success mantra.'"

I couldn't hide my disappointment. "I know everything that happened; I just narrated it all, so haven't I already acknowledged it?"

Nandu saw the disappointment on my face and continued. "Whenever I am unhappy or face a confounding situation, I use my little success mantra. I ask myself: 'Can I accept this?'" Nandini made a bracket with her thumb and index finger.

"That's it? That's the mantra?" I asked in disbelief.

"Yes. Can I accept this? That's the magic mantra!" Nandu replied with a large grin.

I couldn't hide my disappointment. "What? C'mon, Nandu! It just seems a little silly; I don't see how it can help."

Nandu understood my skepticism. "I know this may sound absurd. It may sound like ordinary words. But if these words are used wholeheartedly, this mantra can prove to be very powerful. You will only understand if you truly believe it and see yourself. After all, the proof of the pudding is in the eating. So, the efficacy of this mantra can be known only when you actually apply it in testing situations. Trust me; it can help you accept and overcome every negative situation by dissolving your resistance to the situation. It enables you to accept the situation rather than living in denial."

Nandini gave me a small smile and placed her hand on my shoulder. "This mantra will help you come to terms with the situation, so you can approach it with a calm mind and not get consumed by negative emotions. You must try and find solutions while also using this mantra at the same time. Exercising this mantra makes the mind stable, which helps dissolve resistance. Finding the solution to the problem then becomes easy. In many cases, you may also find that there was no real problem. It was just a resistance to the situation based on some presumption clouding your view."

I couldn't help but feel overwhelmed. "So, what should I do now? How do I even start?" I asked.

"The very first thing to do is to accept whatever has happened. Accept yourself along with all your past mistakes and weaknesses. Accept your situation. Accept your lost opportunities. Accept all the disharmony in your relationships. That is how it is. Once you accept yourself as it is, things will become much easier for you," Nandini said determinedly.

I took a deep breath and tried to take in everything Nandini had said. "You must change the situation if it is wrong, but after unlocking both your hands."

"What do you mean by unlocking both hands?"

"Let me explain," Nandini smiled and continued. "When we try to accomplish any work with one of our hands locked behind, we cannot act efficiently. But we can achieve it far more easily when we act with both our hands unlocked. Similarly, when we resist situations, it is like locking either or both hands. The only problem right now is that noise in your head that is resisting the past. When we accept the way things are, when we embrace our past, our hands are no longer locked, and we can take the right action with an open mind. So, your first step must be to accept the situation. By doing this, you will start looking beyond the grief and the worry that has assailed you through the problem. You will open up to new ways of resolving it. With acceptance, all things will get absorbed easily; they won't get locked within you."

I sat quietly and thought for a moment. Nandini also remained silent, so that I could think.

"Nandu, I realize that there's no other way. I have to accept everything. I accept whatever has happened, and I'm willing to take responsibility for everything I have done and for all those I have hurt."

I couldn't help but tear up a little. I realized that if I were watching everything that had occurred, I would've regarded myself as a terrible person, someone whom I would never want to be around. But Nandini was right. Not all was lost, I could still feel the faint glimmer of hope and the longing to fulfill those dreams that I had set out to achieve. And it was a solace to have people like Nandini who loved me. I finally brought myself to accept everything that had happened wholeheartedly. I finally looked up at Nandini, who looked back at my relieved face.

"At first, it sounds too easy, but it's probably one of the most difficult things I've done," I said with a sigh, thinking back to my night on the roof and asked, "What if I am unable to accept everything? The way things are all going downward. I am not sure whether I can accept being mocked and alienated. I am still a little scared to step back into the social circle, but I must if I can ever get a job again."

"You simply have to accept that you cannot accept it," Nandini smiled.

"What? Doesn't that defeat the purpose of accepting?"

Nandini explained, "Not really. With this mantra, if the answer is, 'No, I cannot accept this,' then you can also accept your non-acceptance. You can tell yourself, 'It's okay; right now, I'm unable to accept this, and that's fine. At the least, I fully accept my inability to accept the situation.'

"The purpose of accepting is to come to terms with the situation, so you are not lying to yourself to protect yourself from reality. If you cannot accept something, then accept that you cannot accept it. You are not obliged to accept everything in the world. Every person is different, and different things are found acceptable for different people. When you accept that you cannot accept the situation, you will be able to come to terms with it."

"How could accepting my negative feelings towards someone I dislike make any difference?"

Nandini seemed to sense my doubt and continued to explain her method, "For example, whenever you see someone you dislike, tell yourself, 'I just can't tolerate this person.' Then ask yourself, 'Can I accept my non-acceptance? Can I accept my current state of mind? Can I accept my mind's intolerance for this person? And what does this convey about me?' Because, after all, when you hate someone else, it affects you first; you have to accept that."

I pondered on her words for a moment. "Could it be true that my negative feelings towards someone else were affecting me more than the other person?"

Nandini continued, "If you are worried and that worry is constantly bugging you, just ask yourself, 'Can I accept this worry?' Your answer will be, 'Yes, I am worried right now. That's the truth of this moment. I can accept it.' If you deny it and reject that you are worried, then you may act recklessly."

I felt relieved as I realized that accepting my negative emotions didn't mean I had to act on them. I could simply acknowledge them and let them go. If they still persisted, I could let them be!

"In this way, when you accept your non-acceptance, something new unfolds and amazes you. Essentially, you say, 'Okay, this is how I am. I have faults, I see flaws in the world around me, but I am fine with how I am. I completely accept myself as I am at this moment. When I start accepting myself, it will be easier for me to accept others along with their faults."

Nandini's words made sense. I had to start by accepting myself before I could accept others. But what if I couldn't accept something? Nandini had an answer for that too.

"It's possible that you will answer negatively in some situations. If that happens, give yourself time and ask, 'Can I accept this?' If you still feel something isn't acceptable, give yourself even more time and ask again, 'Can I accept this now?'"

I realized that accepting something wasn't an instant process but rather a gradual one. And the more I questioned my negative feelings, the easier it would be to accept them.

"You'll see that after some time, a positive answer will emerge. The mind cannot hold resistance for long when you question it consciously. Resistance lives within us in the dark of our non-awareness. The moment resistance is brought to the light of our awareness, it cannot survive for long. This may not come about immediately, but after a few minutes, perhaps a few hours, or maybe even a few days, you'll be able to say yes. Once you're able to accept the situation, you will instantly feel relieved."

Nandini's words gave me hope. If I could learn to accept my negative feelings, maybe I could let go of them and move on. It wasn't an easy process, but it was possible.

"So, to summarize, if you're experiencing a tough time in accepting a situation or individual, you can practice these four steps to help you overcome the situation: Wait for some time and try to accept it again, accept only part of the situation, accept only the negative feeling that the situation has caused, and accept not being able to accept it. This is a very critical step. Ask yourself, 'Can I accept that I cannot accept it?'"

"When you accept something, you release any negative charge associated with it," Nandini continued. "And that's when the magic happens. Your mind begins to shift and accept related and similar issues. You attract positivity towards you."

"All I have to do is review the situation in my mind and ask myself, 'Can I accept this?'" I repeated her words, trying to imprint them into my mind. "And if I can, it should seem lighter and clearer."

Nandini smiled. "Exactly. And if you still feel negative, keep asking yourself until it's completely clear."

7

Everyone Has Struggles

It sounded too good to be true, but I wanted to believe it. I wanted to believe that this simple act of acceptance could change my life. The idea of accepting my non-acceptance was something I had never considered before. It seemed almost counterintuitive, but I was willing to give it a try.

I realized that I once had negative feelings towards Nandini. I had felt that I couldn't tolerate her because of my envy and insecurities. Could I acknowledge the feelings that I once held?

I couldn't help but feel a tinge of insecurity as I listened to Nandini's words of wisdom. Although her advice was invaluable, I couldn't shake off feeling unworthy of her kindness.

Nandini offered her support and guidance to me. But why was she so eager to help me? Was it out of genuine care, or was it just pity for my insecurities?

As I pondered on these thoughts, I felt a pang of guilt for having once harbored terrible thoughts about her. I had let my insecurities and fears cloud my judgment.

I longed to confess my past thoughts to her, to seek her forgiveness and let her know how much I valued her. But I was terrified of rejection. What if she thought less of me for thinking such things about her? What if she didn't believe that I had changed?

I took a deep breath and mustered the courage to speak. "Nandini, I have something to confess. I used to have terrible thoughts about you because of my insecurities. I was jealous of you. I am so sorry."

To my relief, Nandini simply smiled and placed a comforting hand on my shoulder. "Esha, there is nothing to forgive. We all have our insecurities and doubts. It is important that you have accepted them and are willing to work on them. I will always be here to support you, no matter what."

Her words of reassurance touched me deeply, and I felt a sense of relief and gratitude. I realized that my insecurities were just a part of me and that sharing them with those who cared about me was fine. And at that moment, I knew that Nandini was indeed a friend who would always be there for me through thick and thin.

I shifted in my seat, feeling a sudden rush of nervousness. Nandini had been so kind to me since I arrived, but I couldn't help but wonder why she was so eager to help me. I cleared my throat, trying to steady my voice.

"Can I ask you one more thing?" I asked, a little hesitant.

Nandini turned to me with a smile. "Of course, Eshu. What's on your mind?"

I took a deep breath before continuing. "Would you mind sharing what happened to you in the past? When we were young, you were always timid and not very social. But now, the woman before me is confident and wise. Can you share what happened, of course, only if you're comfortable with it?"

Nandini's smile didn't waver as she nodded. "Of course! I have no problem sharing."

As she began to speak, a wave of guilt washed over me. I realized I had made assumptions about her life when we reunited in Mumbai. At the time, I saw how good her life was and told myself she must have just gotten lucky while I hadn't been so fortunate. As she opened up about her financial, health, and relationship troubles, I felt a pang of empathy.

"One day, I realized I was just going with the emotions. I wasn't truly living," Nandini continued. "I was taking classes because I needed to, not because I was interested in the topic. I was going along with things others wanted to do, but I was never truly enjoying myself. I couldn't cope with the pressure when I started my first job."

I listened intently, feeling a sense of unease at the thought of Nandini struggling like this. But as she spoke about her being diagnosed with diabetes and her financial struggles, I felt a lump form in my throat.

"I was devastated," Nandini said softly. "At that time, I had just started my career, and my husband started going back to college for a postgraduate degree. We were financially struggling, and I found myself always crying."

I couldn't believe what I was hearing. Nandini, the woman who seemed to have everything together, had gone through so much. As she spoke about attending a spiritual retreat and learning techniques to manage her emotions, I couldn't help but feel a sense of awe.

"So, your techniques came from this retreat?" I inquired.

"Yes, it's been a series of retreats. During the first one, I learned several techniques that have helped me manage myself better. Before that, I was simply going through the motions, rarely stopping to contemplate the reasons behind my emotions or the potential consequences. So, I went back for more." Nandini explained.

Her words struck me, as I could relate to allowing my emotions to lead the way, often disregarding the consequences in the heat of the moment.

Nandini continued, "I attended the first retreat out of sheer curiosity, but with time, it became my sanctuary, a place where I found inner peace. After that, I started attending weekly follow-up sessions regularly. This helped me smoothly navigate through my daily situations."

As I listened intently, I couldn't help but gaze at Nandini with empathy and a bit of sadness. It dawned on me that I had never known about the struggles she faced in her life. I had assumed that everything was going smoothly for her.

"It's all in the past," Nandini said, seeing the look on my face. "But you know, everyone has problems. My problems were no different than what everyone else was facing. I didn't know how to handle them. But now I know better, and I am happier for it."

She suddenly stood up and cut the tension. "Now, shall we have lunch? I know you have been homesick, so I made some of our classics from back home."

I followed her to the kitchen, my mind still reeling from our conversation. As we sat down to eat, I couldn't help but feel grateful for Nandini's friendship and guidance. And I made a promise to myself to never judge someone based on appearances or assumptions again.

After lunch, as I was about to leave, Nandini walked me to the door. "I'd better be going. I have to get some stuff from the grocery, or else I will have an argument with Reema again," I said.

"Let's keep in touch and meet often. We can talk about everything that is bothering you and figure a way out. I'm sure you will overcome this difficult phase and lead a balanced and beautiful life," Nandini said with a reassuring smile. "How about meeting again this weekend for dinner? You can also meet Anand and Khushi."

"Dinner? That sounds great. I can't wait to meet your family; I bet they're lovely. Thanks for the invite!" I said as I waved goodbye. For the first time in so many weeks, I sensed a faint smile on my lips, which surprised me.

As I stepped out of her apartment building, I felt a sense of calm. But my moment of peace was short-lived when I couldn't find a taxi. Frustration began to set in at that moment, but then I remembered Nandini's words.

I recited her mantra to myself, "Can I accept this?" I realized that I could. I couldn't control the fact that taxis were full, and I couldn't magically make one appear. I took a deep breath and reminded myself that I had other options. I could take public transport. It was a readily available solution, but my anger clouded my judgment. I began walking towards the bus stop, my steps lighter as I shed the burden of frustration.

As I walked, I couldn't help but feel proud of myself for accepting the situation and finding a way to move forward. In the past, I would have let the frustration consume me, ruining my mood for the rest of the day. But now, I felt like I was in control.

Just as I reached the halfway point to the bus stop, I saw an empty taxi and hailed it. I felt grateful for the unexpected stroke of luck, but more importantly, I felt grateful for the lesson I had learned from Nandini. I immediately texted her about my experience, thanking her for the mantra and for being a source of support.

The rest of the day went smoothly. I managed to complete my errands without any further hiccups. As I prepared for bed, I reflected on the events of the day. I realized that the journey toward acceptance was not an easy one, but a necessary one.

8

Mending Broken Bonds

Over the next two days, I thought a lot about what Nandini had taught me. I started using the acceptance mantra in small situations, like when I messed up my lunch or received a mocking comment on my Facebook. I took a moment to contemplate, "Can I accept this?" With the answer yes, I could calmly think of my options. So, what if I mess up an omelet? It simply becomes scrambled eggs. I also decided to ignore the comment on my post. Everyone has their own opinions, but if I respond angrily, it will only escalate the situation. After feeling relieved of the anger, I could go about the day and get some chores done.

The day I had a dinner plan with Nandini, I walked into the kitchen in the morning, where Reema was cheerfully preparing her breakfast. "Good morning, Reema!" I greeted her.

Reema stopped humming and just said, "Hmmm," in a confused and irritated tone.

I didn't like her response and was immediately about to react in a harsh tone. But I held myself back and swallowed my words. Nandini's voice reverberated in my mind - Use the mantra, "Can I accept this?" and accept the situation as it is. "Indeed, I can," I thought to myself with a deep breath. With this, I felt my irritation and anger subsided considerably. After all, it was my fault that our relationship had turned up this way. If I had been in Reema's shoes and someone had treated me the way I treated her, I wouldn't have forgiven them so easily, either. In the past, a trivial argument like this would have spoiled my entire day. I wonder if we could ever be close again, but I knew things won't happen just because I wanted them to.

I joined Nandini's lovely family for dinner that evening. Anand Verma was tall, cheerful, and an easy-going person. He was just as kind and inviting as Nandini. "Hi, Esha! Glad to meet you finally; I've heard a lot about you," he greeted me warmly.

"Hi! I hope you have heard good things," I teased.

"Well, Nandini always tells me the good stuff," he said as we settled at the dining table.

"We were such simple, straightforward, and sweet girls, weren't we, Eshu?" She gave me a playful wink, and I couldn't help but grin in agreement.

"Yes, very simple and sweet," I agreed gleefully.

"Who's this, Mom?" Khushi jumped onto her mother's lap. Khushi was a cute, chubby kid with a ponytail and an endearing pout.

"This is Esha; she's my school friend. You remember Granny's house?" Nandini asked.

Khushi nodded.

"Esha and I were neighbors; her family lived near Granny's. We went to school together, just like you and Divya," Nandini explained.

Khushi's eyes glowed happily, and she gave a shy giggle.

The dinner was heartwarming with Nandini's delectable dishes that tasted just like her mother's, bringing back fond memories of my childhood playing at Nandini's house. As I savored each bite of my favorite mustard greens dish, *Sarson ka saag*, I felt touched by her thoughtfulness and the effort she put into the meal. It was a delightful culinary experience that I thoroughly enjoyed.

After dinner, Nandini and I settled on the couch in her room for a chat, with soft music playing in the background.

I took a deep breath, "Nandu," I began, my voice quivering with insecurity, "You're right. The mind is a powerful tool, and I believe in its potential. But...I'm just not sure if I have the strength to train it. Especially in those really tough situations, you know? When everything seems to be falling apart, it's much easier to deny reality and pretend everything's okay."

As I spoke, my voice trailed off, and I felt a wave of frustration. It was as though I was trapped in an endless loop of negative thoughts and emotions, and I didn't know how to break free. Despite my efforts to use the acceptance mantra, I still felt stuck. It had helped me calm down and view the situation more rationally, but it hadn't alleviated my negative emotions.

I paused; my mind drifted back to that morning's confrontation with Reema. "Take this morning, for example. When Reema brushed off my greetings, I was so upset. I was able to calm myself down using the acceptance mantra, and when I stopped to think about it, I realized that if someone had treated me the way I treated her, I would've been just as upset. It's just so hard to accept the situation for what it really is. It's so much easier to blame her, the argument, or...or anything else, really."

Nandini's features softened as she spoke with deep compassion. "Eshu, it's not as overwhelming as it may seem. Just take small steps, and don't expect too much too soon. Relationships can be complicated, and they take time to build. But as you work on yourself and take things one day at a time, Reema will surely notice the positive changes in you."

As I sat with Nandini, I couldn't help but feel like there was something else I needed to tell her. My eyes drifted to the floor, and I fidgeted with my hands. I had discovered an open bottle of alcohol in the kitchen the day before, and in a moment of weakness, I had taken a few sips to soothe the persistent headache that had plagued me all day. Now, the guilt of my actions weighed heavily on my shoulders. Should I tell Nandini? Would she lose faith in me if she knew?

After much internal debate, I finally mustered the courage to speak. "There's one more thing I wanted to share," I said hesitantly. "I'm ashamed to say this, but I'm addicted to alcohol. I've tried to kick the habit but to no avail. I don't know if I'll ever be free from it."

My voice trailed off, and I let out a disappointed sigh. "It's just... it's difficult to stay away from, especially with all the chaos going on in my life right now. I know it's terrible, but I just can't resist it. Afterward, I felt so guilty. I tried using the acceptance mantra, but honestly, it just made me feel worse. Accepting my actions made me feel even guiltier."

Nandini responded with a comforting tone, "Don't be too hard on yourself. Addiction is not an easy thing to overcome. If it were, everyone would be able to do it quickly. But there are techniques that can help. For example, when you feel the urge to drink, try observing it without reacting. Imagine it like a cloud passing by, and watch it without judgment, resistance, or action. By detaching yourself from any emotional connection to it and viewing it from an outsider's perspective, you'll find that the urge loses power over you. This technique is called mindfulness, an incredibly powerful tool for training the mind."

I pondered Nandini's words for a moment, considering her advice. I wish I had her optimism! "Mindfulness, huh? That sounds interesting. I have heard people say, 'Be mindful.' Is it like that?"

Nandini giggled, explaining, "Mindfulness is a skill that can be learned and developed over time with regular practice. It can increase awareness and focus, reduce stress and anxiety, and improve overall well-being. Observing your thoughts and emotions like a disinterested spectator without reacting to them creates a dissociation between yourself and your mind. Your mind becomes the observed, and your awareness becomes the observer. In this state, you can view your thoughts and emotions objectively, as if you are watching yourself from outside yourself. You realize that they are not you, and you are not them. You are the awareness behind them, and that awareness is always calm, peaceful, and unaffected by the ups and downs of life. When you tap into that awareness, you tap into your true nature, beyond all addictions and distractions."

Her words gave me hope, but I still felt a bit hesitant. "I understand, but do you think I can actually do it? It sounds even harder than the mantra. And what if I still struggle to accept the situation?"

Nandini responded compassionately, "Again, don't be too hard on yourself, Eshu. If you slip up, just observe the situation without judgment and get back on track. Remember, mindfulness is all about being present in the moment rather than dwelling on past or future thoughts. It may take some time and effort, but it's definitely worth it. You know, I've been there too. I had an addiction in the past."

I was taken aback by her words. Nandini had faced her own struggles with addiction and came out the other side. It gave me hope that I could do the same. "Really? Can you tell me more about it?" I asked curiously.

"Sure, I don't mind. I don't feel ashamed about my past because it's a part of who I am today. Do you remember how much I loved sweets as a child?" Nandini chuckled, reminiscing.

I laughed along with her, recalling how much she used to indulge in sugary treats like *Jalebis* and *Rasgullas*. "Yes, of course! You were always raiding the sweet shop with your pocket money."

Nandini nodded in agreement, "Yes, that's right. During my college years, I was under a lot of stress and started relying on sweets as a coping mechanism. I used to eat so many sweets, sometimes even an entire cake in a day, to keep myself going. It was like how some people rely on coffee for energy. But eventually, I ended up in the hospital with dizziness and was diagnosed with diabetes. I had to choose between enjoying sweets in moderation or risking diabetes."

She then shared how she learned about mindfulness, which helped her overcome her addiction to sweets. "I started practicing mindfulness and discovered new ways to satisfy my cravings. For example, did you know that our sense of smell and taste are deeply interconnected? It's believed that about 80% of what we taste actually comes from the smell of the food. That's why some people hold their nose when taking medicine or get a stomach ache when smelling something unpleasant. I could control my sweet cravings by smelling something sweet instead. Whenever I needed energy, I went jogging. And when I craved something sweet, I would light sweet-scented candles. With time, focus, and practice, you can also distance yourself from alcohol and figure out how to overcome it. Practice mindfulness now; later, we can discuss rewiring."

9

The 3D Formula

It was an intriguing idea that had never crossed my mind before. I was fascinated by the concept of quelling one's craving by replacing it with something entirely different, especially something healthy. "What about my alcoholism?" I pondered aloud. I don't even know if I can replace it with anything since I don't even know why I drink.

Nandini responded, "Of course, you can do it too. It'll just take some practice. You don't necessarily have to replace it with something else; that was the simplest way for me to wean myself off sweets. We can train the mind by using a technique called the 3D formula. It consists of three steps: Detachment, Declaration, and Delayed Gratification. That's how I managed to distance myself from overeating sweets."

Seating herself beside me, Nandini continued, "Firstly, detachment is crucial. You must detach yourself from the compulsion to satisfy your desires. The urges you experience are not inherent ones like hunger, thirst, or the need for shelter. These are self-created cravings, a means for you to escape reality, am I right? If you think about it carefully, many people occasionally drink without it becoming an addiction. In many countries, people have a glass of wine with dinner or a can of beer at a rare sports event. But they do not form an alcohol addiction, so have you considered why you have?"

Nandini's words sparked a deep reflection within me. It did begin as an occasional indulgence, but it gradually became a habitual part of my life. I couldn't help but wonder why. Even my friends, who drank and partied alongside me, never seemed to develop the same attachment. Was I simply unlucky in comparison, or was something inherently wrong with me? "You're right," I confessed, "I've been actively trying to detach myself from alcohol. I haven't stepped my foot in a bar recently and have been trying my hardest to avoid it. But sometimes, I just can't help it. No matter how much it has ruined my life, it just makes dealing with my problems easier."

Nandini looked at me and said, "That's an excellent first step, but detachment encompasses more than that. In the 3D formula, detachment entails freeing yourself from the need to indulge your senses. Through mindfulness, you can establish a dialogue with yourself, engaging in introspective conversations. By asking pertinent questions, you can gain a heightened awareness of the situation and its underlying causes. Have you asked yourself why it seems to make it easier to deal with your problems? What exactly happens within you when you get these bouts of craving for alcohol? Why have quick-fix solutions ended up creating more problems for you? When you consciously ask such introspective questions to your mind, you get the opportunity to step back from your compulsive behavior and watch it deeply."

Curious, I inquired, "How can I question my mind?"

"There are various ways to approach it," Nandini began. "Let me ask you, Esha: Do you perceive yourself as a body housing a mind, as a mind enveloped by a body, or as a conscious presence accompanied by a body-and-mind? If you believe you are a body with a mind confined within it, you will never have control over your sensory cravings. When you view yourself as a mind encompassed by a body, you can learn to govern the body and restrain the senses. But when you experience yourself as the conscious presence that exists apart from your body and mind, you gain mastery over your mind as well as the body.

"When I questioned why I relied so heavily on sweets, I realized it provided a pleasurable sensation. When I reflected further, I understood that the addiction wasn't to the sweets themselves but to the surge of energy they provided. However, it's important to understand that it's perfectly acceptable for your mind to experience various states, whether it's tiredness, restlessness, or sadness. You don't always need to seek a solution; sometimes, you can simply allow yourself to go through those emotions, remembering that they are temporary."

I raised an important question, "But doesn't the mind send those emotions as signals to prompt us into action? Like when you feel hungry, it's a clear sign that it's time to eat. And when you're restless or stressed, it usually indicates a need to do something about it, right?"

Nandini responded, providing a fresh perspective, "When it comes to hunger, it's crucial to listen to your body's cues. However, restlessness and stress operate differently. Stress is essentially your body's response to a perceived threat, which can make you feel restless. In situations where your body senses a threat, it triggers the fight-or-flight response. This activates the release of appropriate hormones, such as adrenaline, providing a temporary surge of energy that allows you to push beyond your usual physical limits. For example, if a lion is chasing you, you won't stop running just because you're tired; the adrenaline coursing through your veins keeps you going.

"In modern times, our minds often associate stress with less threatening situations due to our learned associations. While our ancestors experienced stress as a response to immediate danger, we now experience similar physiological reactions to events like public speaking. However, practicing mindfulness and engaging in a dialogue with your mind can give insights into why a particular situation is causing stress. For instance, if you perform poorly in a speech, you might fear losing your job, impacting your ability to pay rent and buy food. It's in this context that the situation may feel threatening. Or it could be due to the fear of being ridiculed that relates to a painful memory from childhood. However, once you recognize and understand this perspective, you can reframe your thinking and realize that it's not something to be overly concerned about. This understanding can effectively alleviate restlessness and reduce stress levels."

I took a moment to absorb everything, realizing the extent to which I had created this addiction myself. At first, I did not desire to drink, but I convinced myself that I needed it to navigate the corporate world and cover up my guilt. Over time, drinking became a crutch; it helped me drown out the thoughts of guilt and voices telling me to change in my head. Even when I suffered from headaches caused by drinking, my mind tricked me into thinking that more alcohol was the solution. The loud music and party atmosphere distracted me from the reality of my situation. I realized that I needed to embrace mindfulness to gain a deeper understanding of my actions and motivations.

"I understand, Nandu," I confessed, a mix of determination and vulnerability in my voice. "I will start practicing mindfulness. But what are the other two parts of the 3D formula?"

Nandini smiled, appreciating my eagerness. "It's wonderful to see your enthusiasm. You'll gradually get the hang of it. The second step is Declaration. This method involves verbally accepting and announcing your intentions to your body and mind. Let's say you have a daily habit of drinking coffee but want to break free from it because you know caffeine is detrimental to your health. Without a clear declaration, your body and mind may not fully grasp your desire to change. It's important to give them a distinct command and consistent practice."

Curiosity sparked within me. "Why wouldn't the body and mind understand without a declaration? Isn't that how the mind typically operates?"

Nandini began to explain, delving into the science behind our mind's functioning. "In a way, our experiences and beliefs shape the mind's wiring. The transfer and processing of information occur in the nervous system, which comprises cells called neurons. These neurons form connections with other neurons to send and receive information, and the number of these connections depends on the significance we attach to certain experiences or beliefs, which strengthens our memory of that experience or belief. This phenomenon is called neuroplasticity in the scientific realm, as these connections constantly evolve."

"For instance, when a child sees a dog for the first time, their mind stores an image of it as a memory. Now, let's say the child comes across a video where a cat's meow is dubbed over the image of a dog. Their mind creates a new sound memory and links it to the dog's image. Over time, if the child hears a cat's meow while looking at a picture of a dog, they may gradually believe that dogs meow instead of bark. However, this isn't a permanent state. When the child starts school, and other kids inform them that dogs bark, it establishes a new connection with the sound of barking to the image of the dog. Meeting a barking dog further reinforces the correct understanding. This is how learning occurs, and children adapt more swiftly because they have fewer pre-existing connections, allowing their minds to rewire more readily. You, too, can learn to rewire your mind, but it begins with making a declaration for both your body and mind to follow and then staying committed to that declaration."

"I understand. So, if I firmly declare my intention to stop drinking, will my mind start to change?"

Nandini paused to think and then explained, "It's a good starting point, but it's not that simple. Once you detach from your addiction and gain a better understanding of it, you can take the next step. Declare your intention to alter the way your brain links alcohol with pleasure. Alcoholism is more complex than your addiction, so let me explain why alcohol feels good.

"When something brings you pleasure, it activates a brain system called the reward pathways. These pathways release chemicals that make you feel good and reinforce the behavior. That's why you may find yourself needing more drinks to achieve the same feeling as your brain becomes accustomed to it. Different people find pleasure in different things because they activate their unique reward pathways. The more you engage in a behavior, the stronger the connection becomes, and you need more of it to experience pleasure again. This creates a cycle where it becomes harder to feel the initial pleasure you seek. However, if you abruptly stop drinking, your mind may feel unsettled because it has associated drinking with satisfaction in certain situations.

"By changing your mindset to believe that drinking isn't connected to those positive feelings, you'll gradually lose the desire to drink in those situations. For example, imagine a corporate party where you used to drink to fit in. Drinking became linked to social acceptance in your mind. But by breaking that association between drinking and fitting in, you won't feel the need to drink anymore. This transformation takes time, practice, and, most importantly, patience."

"I now understand better why I keep drinking, but I still have many questions. How long will it take to change my thinking? And how will I know when my thinking has successfully changed?"

"Ah, now we come to the third step: Delayed Gratification. This step involves actively postponing the fulfillment of your urges. Let's take the example of overeating—an unhealthy habit where one indulges whenever the urge arises. Now, imagine feeling the impulse to grab a handful of chips. Instead of giving in immediately, set a timer for 10 minutes. Do you still feel the same urge after the time has passed? Most likely not, as your hunger was not genuine but a mere craving. By allowing yourself the chips only after the designated time, you break the cycle of associating food with immediate gratification. Instead, you learn to eat only when it is truly appropriate."

"So, if I understand correctly, when I feel the urge to drink because of loneliness, and I manage to resist momentarily before giving in, I will no longer see drinking as a solution to my loneliness?"

"Exactly! Give it a try the next time you feel the urge to drink. If you find it challenging to resist internally, set a physical timer for 10 or 15 minutes. This will allow you to reflect on your thoughts and reasoning. When the time is up, you will realize that drinking was never a genuine solution to loneliness. It was merely a distraction, as there are numerous other ways to address it, such as reaching out to a friend or engaging with family. By doing so, you gradually weaken the connections between alcohol and loneliness while strengthening the associations between seeking support from others and experiencing a sense of fulfillment.

"Once you start applying these strategies, you can take them a step further by replacing bad habits with healthier alternatives. Like how instead of indulging in sweets, I started exercising to get the energy boost I needed. When I had intense cravings for the satisfying feeling of eating sweets, I turned to sweet scents instead of desserts."

"So, since alcohol helped me ignore my stresses and problems, can I try replacing it with something else that makes me calm?"

"That depends on what you discover as you go through the process of detachment. If you find that alcohol helps calm your mind, many people have found that journaling can have a similar effect. If you feel like alcohol fills a void of loneliness, you can try seeking more support from friends. It really comes down to understanding yourself better. Take it slow, accept that it can take time, gradually incorporate these practices, and you'll gain insight into what works for you. But I think that's enough food for the mind today," Nandini said, chuckling as she noticed me processing all the information she had just shared.

"Indeed, I have a lot to contemplate tonight. Perhaps writing in a journal will help me make sense of everything and allow me to express my emotions on paper in a private and personal way."

Khushi entered the room and settled on Nandini's lap, "Mummy, I'm feeling sleepy."

As I bid my farewells and began my journey home, my mind swirled with the overwhelming amount of knowledge I had just learned. It was a lot to take in, and I couldn't help but doubt my ability to put it all into practice. Let's face it; my challenges weren't limited to just one problem; many areas of my life needed improvement. Nevertheless, there was solace in knowing that Nandini believed in me, even though I struggled to believe in myself. I couldn't help but wonder if I would ever regain the confidence I once had.

10

No Pain, No Gain

In a rush, I hurried back to my room as the darkness settled in. Considering my options, I decided to skip ordering takeout and settled for a simple snack—just a banana and a glass of milk. Surprisingly, this small choice brought me a sense of happiness. Eating the banana made me feel healthier compared to indulging in fast food.

Once in my room, I grabbed an empty notebook, eager to jot down the changes I wanted to make in my life. These changes included overcoming my addiction to alcohol, controlling my urge to party, adopting healthier eating habits, and improving my relationships. I carefully wrote down everything Nandini had taught me.

Nandini emphasized the importance of accepting the things that had happened by using the acceptance mantra. This process would help me clear my mind and rely more on logical thinking rather than being overwhelmed by emotions. Even if there were situations I couldn't fully accept, acknowledging my struggle would still bring me clarity.

Next, I learned about the 3D technique: Detachment, declaration, and delayed gratification. By practicing mindfulness, I could have honest conversations with myself to understand why I was so attached to alcohol and find ways to break that attachment. Making declarations would kickstart the changes in my thoughts and behaviors, rewiring my mind to disconnect alcohol from positive feelings. Lastly, I could gradually distance myself from my addictions by practicing delayed gratification. This meant giving myself some time between feeling the urge to indulge and actually satisfying that urge.

Determined to make a positive change, I flipped over to the next page and began writing down my thoughts and aspirations. It was a moment of reflection, realizing that I had unintentionally become dependent on alcohol to cope with my problems.

I couldn't pinpoint exactly when the addiction took hold, but I had convinced myself that drinking was a necessity. Despite my initial reluctance, curiosity got the best of me, and I found myself reaching for that bottle. Drinking seemed to silence the inner voice of my conscience that guided me toward wise decisions, allowing me to ignore the consequences of my actions.

Looking back, it was my own insecurities that led me down this path of addiction. Nandini had made an important point: Many people drink occasionally without getting addicted. I thought this was because they didn't convince themselves that it was a necessity. It's similar to indulging in sweets; most people enjoy them in moderation, but those who convince themselves they need them might end up struggling with self-control.

When others advised me to quit drinking, it stirred up anger within me because, deep down, it echoed what my inner self was trying to tell me. It was easier to direct that anger outward rather than confront my own actions. I realized that it was a misguided coping mechanism that spiraled my life out of control by focusing on temporary solutions while neglecting the larger issues. However, I was ready to accept that I was wrong, despite the pain it brought.

Reflecting on my past choices, I recognized a similar pattern in my pursuit of fitting in through partying. Most people didn't engage in those behaviors and yet managed to belong. In reality, my curiosity and insecurities convinced me that I was doing it to conform instead of accepting the reality that I was curious, leading to addiction. Loneliness and a lack of control in a new environment fueled my insecurities, driving me to seek solace in destructive habits.

Even when it came to my eating habits, I convinced myself that I didn't have time to prioritize healthy meals, using time contracts as an excuse. However, observing others around me, it became evident that time was not the issue—I was simply making excuses for my own laziness. I understood that it would require significant time and effort to rewire my mind to recognize that I didn't need these harmful behaviors in my life.

I had to find alternative ways to fulfill the cravings and urges I'd become addicted to. As a starting point, I planned to substitute alcohol with beverages like tea, coffee, or juice, even though they might contain caffeine or sugar. It's a step towards gradually distancing myself from alcohol. On top of that, drinks could make us feel full without all the added carbs. If I could master mindfulness, I won't need to find ways to silence the voices in my mind; instead, I could engage in meaningful conversations with myself, gaining a better understanding of my thoughts and emotions.

After pouring my heart onto the pages of my notebook and confronting my behaviors and justifications, I felt an overwhelming headache. The process of introspection and acceptance made me feel vulnerable and mentally exhausted. However, I recognized the necessity of embarking on this journey. It reminded me of the saying, "No pain, no gain." Coming to terms with everything won't be easy, and making amends for my past actions would be challenging.

At times, the idea of escaping and starting fresh somewhere else, surrounded by new people, seemed tempting. But deep down, I knew that unless I addressed my underlying issues, I'd likely repeat the same mistakes elsewhere. I realized that I was trapped in this situation and must take responsibility for fixing myself and my life. Yes, it would undoubtedly be painful, but the rewards of personal growth and transformation were undoubtedly worth the effort. I realized that I needed to face the pain and transcend it. No gain without understanding pain!

The road ahead might be difficult, but I knew that by confronting my past, embracing change, and making positive choices, I could build a future that was free from the chains of addiction and filled with genuine happiness and fulfillment. Despite the pain from my headache, I took solace in the knowledge I gained about myself that day and was ready for further growth. With that in mind, I drifted off to sleep.

11

An Opportunity Knocks

It had been a week since my dinner with Nandini and her family, and I had been actively applying the techniques she shared with me. We met once more during the week to meditate together, and I was getting better at staying focused and practicing mindfulness. With some free time on my hands, I started reflecting on my life and thinking about ways to improve myself.

Suddenly, Nandini called me with excitement in her voice, "Hey, Esha! I hope you're having a great day. Can we meet up for coffee in an hour? I have an amazing opportunity for you!" Her voice was so full of energy.

Her excitement was contagious, and I couldn't help but giggle, "Of course! I'm looking forward to seeing you later."

It had been a while since I felt excited about dressing up. Ever since I started gaining weight, I lost interest in fashion. After the call, I felt renewed enthusiasm as I got ready to go out. I enjoyed thinking about designs and styles again. I hummed to myself as I got ready and headed out.

We met at a cute coffee shop and ordered our drinks. Being health conscious, Nandini got a smoothie while I treated myself to a mocha.

As we sat down, Nandini couldn't contain her excitement any longer, "There's a job opportunity that just came up, and I think it's perfect for you. It's with a client I know well. She owns a high-end boutique and is looking for someone to design formal Indo-Western wear and be a personal stylist for that category. Since you're not currently employed, she wants to see your designs first. If she's impressed, she'll consider you for an interview. I'll email you all the details about this."

I felt grateful for the opportunity, but I couldn't help feeling a bit nervous. I shared my concerns, "Thanks for thinking of me, Nandu. But I'm worried they won't consider my designs. Some companies have turned me down after doing background checks because of my reputation."

Nandini giggled and reassured me, "Don't worry about that. I know this client personally, and if your designs impress her, your skills will speak for themselves."

Still unsure, I expressed my doubts, "But can I really do it? I specialize in formal wear, not Indo-Western attire. The motivations and target audience for those clothes are different."

Nandini's confidence in me was unwavering as she replied, "I truly believe in you. Remember, when we were in college, we didn't know which sector of the industry we would end up in—formal or casual wear. But we adapted and learned on the job. This is similar. Even though you're not experienced in designing casual wear, you have the designing and research skills to succeed."

"Thank you, Nandini; I will surely give it a try."

As we were talking, a question popped into my head. I wondered how Nandini could drink a sweet smoothie when she had struggled with overeating sweets before. Shouldn't she be avoiding them to prevent a relapse? I hesitated momentarily, then asked, "Hey, Nandini... Shouldn't you stay away from sweet things?"

Nandini was taken aback by my question and burst into laughter, almost spilling her drink. "Oh, Esha, you crack me up," she chuckled, trying to catch her breath. "Did you forget that I treated myself to a sweet dessert that night we had dinner? I don't have to completely give up sweets anymore. I've reached a point where I can enjoy them without going overboard. They're just like any other food to me now."

Her face suddenly turned serious. She paused and then continued, "But you know what? Your journey with alcohol might not lead you to a similar place right away. You may need to give yourself time to unshackle yourself from the compulsion. It is only then that you might have a drink occasionally without it taking over your life."

Her words made me pause and think. It made me consider the possibility of finding a balance and regaining control over my relationship with alcohol. Maybe one day, I could enjoy a drink without it becoming a problem. But first, I needed to get rid of the habit of depending on alcohol as an escape mechanism. Nandini's story showed me that change was possible and that I had the power to reshape my habits in a healthier way.

12

Trapped in a Maelstrom

As the deadline for my design submissions drew near, I poured my heart and soul into meticulously perfecting every detail. It had been a challenging two weeks, stepping out of my comfort zone and pushing the boundaries of my creativity. But the results were undeniably remarkable, and a surge of excitement coursed through my veins as I finally clicked the submit button. A sense of accomplishment and anticipation filled every fiber of my being. These designs were more than just pieces of art; they were a testament to my growth and talent.

Brimming with enthusiasm, I hurriedly made my way to Reema's room, eager to share the exhilarating news with my dear friend. However, as I approached her door, a sinking feeling settled in the pit of my stomach. Reality crashed over me like a relentless wave – we were no longer friends. The memory of a recent argument, seemingly trivial, about groceries now loomed large in my mind. In the heat of the moment, Reema had inadvertently touched upon my past mistakes, igniting a firestorm of emotions I couldn't control. Deep down, I knew it was my fault, and a heavy burden of guilt weighed upon my shoulders.

In the aftermath of our heated exchange, I took the opportunity to reflect on my actions. It wasn't until Reema decided to spend some time with her fiancée during the weekend, seeking solace and distance, that the full weight of my behavior hit me like a ton of bricks. Regret washed over me in relentless waves, and I immediately reached out to her, offering a heartfelt apology. Reema assured me that everything was fine, but an underlying tension lingered in the air, hinting that true forgiveness had not yet been granted. The separation only intensified my self-condemnation, and I couldn't help but question the progress I had made. It felt as though, in a mere moment, I had regressed into the same old patterns. Doubts began to gnaw at the very core of my being, whispering insidiously that perhaps the change was nothing more than an elusive dream and that the person I yearned to become was forever out of reach.

A tsunami of panic surged within me, threatening to engulf my entire existence. It felt as though the walls were closing in, constricting my every breath. Gasping for air, I clutched my chest, desperately attempting to regain control over the wild cadence of my racing heart. But the panic attack raged on, unyielding in its torment of my fragile state of mind.

Tears streamed down my face as I found myself crumpled on the floor, ensnared by the grip of despair. Negative thoughts slithered through the labyrinthine corridors of my mind, poisoning any glimmer of hope or progress I had nurtured. The weight of guilt and self-doubt pressed upon me like a leaden shroud, suffocating the spark within me. Doubts echoed mercilessly, repeating the painful refrain that had haunted me for far too long: "Maybe I can never change. Maybe this is just who I truly am."

Time lost all meaning as the panic attack waged its relentless assault, warping my perception of reality. Each passing second stretched into an agonizing eternity, intensifying the suffocating grip of impending doom. Darkness descended, obfuscating the boundaries between the tangible world and the tempestuous whirlwind of emotions churning within me. I felt as though I had descended into the abyss of my own mind, trapped in a maelstrom of powerlessness.

In that dark and tumultuous moment, the urge to call Nandini, my trusted confidante, tugged at my thoughts. But I felt a twinge of guilt, holding me back. I couldn't burden her with my overwhelming despair. I believed that reaching out to Nandini about my current state would only burden her further. Doubts gnawed at my conscience, convincing me that I was a failure who couldn't fix any of my past mistakes. I had been too much of a coward to seek forgiveness from my parents, my attempts at finding a new job seemed futile, and my unhealthy eating habits persisted. To make matters worse, my relationship with Reema had regressed into a hostile state. The weight of these failures compounded, and I couldn't shake off the overwhelming feeling that I was unworthy of Nandini's time and support.

As hours slipped away, I remained sprawled on the floor, physically and mentally drained. Reema unexpectedly walked into the room in this state of despair. Confusion etched across her face as she turned on the light, only to find me in disarray on the floor. Her words trailed off as our eyes locked, both of us at a loss for what to say. I knew I should apologize and accept responsibility for my actions, but the exhaustion had rendered me speechless.

Reema, too, struggled to find the right words. She seemed torn between concern and uncertainty, silently deliberating her next move. Finally, she sat beside me, neither of us uttering a word. The silence hung heavy in the air, laden with unspoken emotions.

Once again I was overwhelmed with guilt, realizing that Reema's expression was one of sadness and worry. This was not the outcome I had desired; I hadn't intended for her to feel sorry for me. All I had wanted was to mend our friendship, but instead, my actions had left her feeling burdened and disheartened. My thoughts raced back to our argument, replaying the moment when I had allowed a petty disagreement to overshadow our bond, ruining her weekend plans. The image of her hurt expression burned into my memory, a constant reminder of the pain I had caused. How could I have let something so trivial escalate to such a destructive extent? I had allowed my own insecurities and unresolved issues to taint our friendship, and now the consequences were staring me in the face. The weight of my shortcomings and the pain I inflicted upon her overwhelmed me.

Though Reema's presence offered a glimmer of solace, it couldn't alleviate the remorse that consumed me. I longed to express my regrets and assure her that I was committed to changing, to becoming a better person. Yet, at that moment, the words eluded me, trapped within the labyrinth of my tangled emotions.

I yearned to turn back time, to rewind to that moment when the argument began, and choose a different path. I wished I could find the strength to control my anger, to respond with compassion and understanding instead of lashing out in defensiveness. Regret seeped into every corner of my being, and I couldn't help but wonder if it was too late to salvage what we had lost.

But alongside regret, a glimmer of hope flickered within me. Despite the weight of our shared silence, Reema's presence signaled a sliver of willingness to bridge the gap between us. It was a fragile thread, susceptible to snapping under the weight of unspoken words and unresolved emotions, but it held the potential for healing.

Together, we sat in that hushed stillness, two souls grappling with unspoken apologies, unvoiced concerns, and the shattered fragments of our friendship.

13

Struggling Between Past and Future

Reema and I eventually found ourselves lying on the floor together after some time. The weight of silence hung heavily between us.

Reema whispered my name in a hushed voice, unsure if I was still awake. Fear gripped me, preventing any response. I dreaded what she might say. Assuming I was asleep, she proceeded cautiously, "I forgive you," she uttered before succumbing to sleep beside me on the floor.

Tears streamed down my face once again. How could she forgive me? The weight of shame was overwhelming. Our fractured friendship had been slowly on the mend even before our argument. Reema was excitedly sharing her plans for the weekend with Rohit, her fiancée, and yet, due to a petty disagreement, I had shattered it all. The trust we had been rebuilding crumbled in an instant. The expression on Reema's face after my outburst still haunted me—not one of sadness, but of regret. She regretted placing her faith in my ability to change, not to hurt her again, and to give me another chance. And now, here I was, seeking forgiveness once more, pleading for a third chance. How could she forgive me so readily? I didn't deserve her forgiveness after the way I exploded at her.

I didn't believe I had any tears left to shed. I thought I had cried them all out. In a barely audible voice, I whispered, "Thank you," though I doubt she heard me amidst her deep slumber. But I couldn't stop expressing my gratitude until sleep finally overtook me as well.

The next morning, I rose first, burdened with exhaustion. It felt as if I had endured an intense workout, though I couldn't recall the last time I had exercised.

Mindful not to disturb Reema, I readied myself and prepared a simple, healthy breakfast for both of us. When Reema awoke, she went about her routine of brushing her teeth and washing her face. As we sat down together, the air between us remained awkwardly heavy. Where should I begin? Should I admit that I overheard her last night? She had only forgiven me because she believed I hadn't heard her words. We sat there in a strained silence, both uncertain about who should initiate the conversation. I didn't want to push her if she wasn't ready.

Time passed, and we finished our meal without exchanging a word. Reema stood up to leave but paused, her voice tinged with expectation, "Aren't you going to say anything to me?"

Tears welled up again, and with a quivering voice, I responded, "I'm so sorry, Reema. I don't know what came over me. I couldn't control my emotions. But I should never have verbally attacked you like that."

Reema paused, sinking back into her seat. "Thank you for apologizing, but that's not what concerns me. What happened last night? Do you have any idea how terrified I was? When I saw you lying motionless on the floor, I was consumed by fear. You didn't move or respond. For a moment, I thought you were dead. Do you realize how terrified I felt?"

I lowered my gaze, unsure of how to respond, as Reema continued to express her thoughts. "And this entire morning, I've been waiting for you to take the initiative. You asked for a second chance, yet it always feels like I have to be the one to start the conversation."

"I'm sorry, Reema," I whispered, fear tightening its grip on me. "I'm just scared that if I reach out first, I might push you when you're not ready. I don't want you to feel like I am pressuring you. I want both of us to feel comfortable around each other."

"Esha, I'm scared of you," Reema uttered hesitantly. "I'm scared of getting hurt by you. I know what happened that night on the rooftop. I didn't mean to overhear, but I caught fragments of your conversation with your friend. Since then, I've lived in constant fear of what you might do. I tried responding to your greetings because I didn't want to be the trigger that pushes you over the edge. Even yesterday, I was supposed to have a nice time with Rohit but returned because I was afraid of what you might do. Despite our current situation, I still hold onto memories of the good times we shared, and I genuinely want what's best for you. However, it's not fair that I have to live in constant fear. I'm afraid that if I accept your friendship again, I'll be dragged back into all the past drama. On the other hand, if I don't, I might be the final straw that pushes you over the edge. When I saw you starting to change, I thought I could trust you not to hurt me. But that argument yesterday, when you exploded at me like that, has left me even more lost. I forgive you for the argument, but I don't know if we can ever be friends again if I have to live in constant worry. If you truly believe you can change, I'm willing to give this another chance. But mere words of wanting to change won't be enough to convince me. I need to see the actual change from you."

I kept my gaze fixed on the ground, overwhelmed by a mix of emotions. I desperately wanted to break free from the shackles of my past behavior and show her that I had transformed, but my inability to communicate my thoughts and emotions effectively only seemed to perpetuate the cycle.

Reema let out a weary sigh. "Esha, if you remain silent, this becomes less of a conversation and more of a one-sided lecture." Her eyes never left mine, yet I struggled to find the words to respond. "I've been putting up emotional barriers because I'm scared of being hurt by you. That's why I find it difficult to share my feelings with you. But you're also putting up barriers of your own. You've only responded and apologized this past week, but what have I gained from these discussions? You haven't truly expressed yourself. I need you to open up to me. Yes, you're afraid of hurting me, but your silence is causing me pain right now. It feels like we're reverting to those chaotic times when I would lecture you. Back then, you would yell at me, and now you're sitting here silently. But nothing has truly changed; I am still having one-sided lectures. Even now, it feels like I'm dictating what you should do because I'm genuinely concerned about you, but I don't think my words are getting through."

The words felt heavy on my tongue, but I knew I had to speak. This was my last chance to make things right with Reema, and the fear of saying the wrong thing consumed me. I grabbed the cup of juice in front of me and chugged it down, finding some semblance of courage to speak my mind.

"I'm genuinely sorry, Reema. I truly am trying to change. I know I don't have much to show for it yet, but I submitted designs for another job opportunity just yesterday. I've been actively working on changing myself. I've been using the techniques Nandini taught me, writing out my plans for the future, and reflecting on rebuilding my relationships. I'm putting in the effort to get everything back to the way it was."

I could sense Reema's hesitation. She, too, downed her juice in one go before speaking her mind. "I think I understand what's going on here, but I'm afraid that if I say it, you'll explode again," she paused briefly, her face revealing a mix of concern and determination, "I'll just come out and say it. You haven't changed at all. You're still trying to control every aspect of your life and living in fear. You're attempting to rewrite the past and return to how things were, but that's not what I want. Back then, you lived in fear and used alcohol and parties to numb yourself. Now, you're doing the same with these techniques. You're still living in fear and trying to exert control over everything. You're moving backward instead of forward. Saying you want to change won't be enough unless you undergo a fundamental transformation."

Rage surged through me. How could she have the audacity to claim that I haven't changed? I've been tirelessly working on self-improvement, so what does she really know? Her life has been a breeze, untouched by the struggles I've endured. I was ready to unleash my fury until I caught sight of Reema's expressionless face. At that moment, I hesitated. It was clear that she genuinely expressed her concern, but her emotionless face showed that she was prepared for any reaction from me. Whether I accepted my faults or lashed out, she had steeled herself to bid me farewell forever if necessary. This was the moment of truth. I had to confront myself brutally and honestly.

She was right. I could not rely on others to fix me. Everyone had their own challenges and burdens to bear. Just as I remained oblivious to Nandini's struggles, assuming her life was a breeze, I made the same mistake with Reema. I overlooked the fact that I was one of the hurdles she had to overcome. She used me as a catalyst for growth and establishing boundaries while I tried to use her to regress and turn back time. Uncomfortable as it was, she was undeniably correct. The truth stung, but I had to accept it. I hadn't truly changed. I'd been telling myself that change was what I should strive for rather than what I genuinely desired. It's time to scrutinize myself more deeply.

Since childhood, I'd been entranced by the glamor and fascination of movies, longing for the opulence and elegance they portrayed.

However, those films only scratched the surface of reality, neglecting the tireless hours of hard work and the complexities of relationships. I realized that I couldn't view myself as the sole protagonist of my own story; rather, I was a character intertwined with others' narratives. Everyone was the main character of their own journey. I couldn't turn back time or dwell in the past. Moving forward was my only option. People won't simply forget my past actions; they could only learn to accept them and move forward. I couldn't expect forgiveness from others just because I was making an effort. It's their choice whether to grant it or not. All I could do was humbly request their patience.

"You're right. I'm scared, Reema. I realize now that I've been trying to mend our friendship, not to fix it, but to return to the past when everything was easier. And that needs to change. I have to shift my mindset. It's true—I've been trying to go back in time. You know me so well; sometimes, it feels like you know me better than I know myself. I genuinely apologize, and I promise to work on myself. Can you please hold on and wait for me? Even if we can't fully mend our past friendship, can we be acquaintances for now? I'll keep striving to better myself. I want to continue greeting you and occasionally share meals. I understand it's your choice, and I know my life will be a mess for a while. I have to literally fix everything about my life and mindset. I now understand that I wasn't wholeheartedly pursuing happiness—I was merely trying to rewrite the past. That's why thinking too hard about it gave me headaches; I didn't want to accept the truth. So, thank you. Despite all the hurt I've caused you, here you are, still trying to help me."

Reema giggled, her laughter carrying a mix of fondness and understanding. "I guess I just have a soft spot for you. Before we became roommates, I always looked up to you. Despite being just a little older, your designs were always eye-catching, and you swiftly made a name for yourself in the industry. I thought you could be my role model, but that image shattered quite quickly. However, I still want to maintain some kind of connection with you. While I'm not sure if we can truly go back to being friends, I want you to know that I'll still be there for you. I don't want to bear the responsibility for you, but I'm willing to keep an acquaintance-like relationship." Reema rose from her seat and extended her hand toward me. "Esha, I genuinely wish you all the luck in finding happiness."

Her words touched a chord within me, and a warm smile spread across my face as I clasped her hand. "Thank you, Reema. Your support means a lot to me. I'm grateful for this opportunity to rebuild our connection, even if it's not the same as before. I understand that the responsibility lies with me to make the necessary changes in my life. I promise to keep working on myself and strive to be a better person. And who knows, maybe our friendship will naturally evolve over time. But for now, let's embark on this acquaintance journey together and see where it takes us."

We released each other's hands, a newfound sense of hope and understanding in the air. The path ahead may be uncertain, but with a willingness to change and a supportive presence by my side, I knew I had a chance at rediscovering happiness and forging a healthier connection with Reema.

14

Breaking Free from Fear

I called Nandini and requested a meeting later that day. On my way to her house, my thoughts raced with the realizations that had dawned on me recently. It amazed me how blind I had been to the extent of my insecurities.

Just a day ago, I had been consumed by fear, contemplating whether or not to confide in Nandini about my panic attack, which only made things worse. Instead, I found myself lying on the floor, paralyzed by fear and pain. I worried that Nandini might think I hadn't been earnestly practicing the techniques or I was beyond help. Reema was right about fear controlling my life. However, there was nothing to fear. As long as Nandini believed in me, she wouldn't abandon me. And even if she did, I would accept it and move forward. Living in fear of endless possibilities was futile; in reality, Nandini would most likely offer comfort and support. As I sighed, this realization sank in deeply. I urgently needed to break free from the grip of fear. As Reema pointed out, I consistently made decisions rooted in fear, relying on external sources such as alcohol, partying, and even Nandini as a coping mechanism instead of a proper support system. I had to learn to depend on my own coping mechanisms and live accordingly.

Nandini welcomed me inside, and we settled in her living room.

"Esha, is something wrong? You seem different today," Nandini remarked, catching me off guard.

Surprised, I chuckled awkwardly and replied, "Was I acting strange? Sorry, a lot has happened recently."

Nandini reassured me, saying, "You can share anything whenever you're ready."

"I know, Nandini. Today, I realized the mistakes I've been making. I've been living in fear all this time. Whenever I failed to apply the techniques you taught me, I hesitated to be honest with you because I feared disappointing you."

Nandini empathetically responded, "I would never be disappointed. Trust me. I understand how difficult it can be. It took me a long time to cultivate self-confidence. I truly comprehend the struggle."

Laughing, I noticed Nandini's genuine surprise, which made everything feel more natural. Nandini was just an ordinary person like everyone else. Throughout this time, I hadn't treated her like a friend but had put her on a pedestal, treating her more like a free therapist.

"Thank you, Nandini. After talking to Reema, I realized that I've been trying to go back to how things were rather than accepting what happened and moving forward. Even with you, I've been using you as a coping mechanism instead of recognizing you as a friend," I confessed. I recounted everything that had transpired the previous weekend, describing how I had grown closer to mending my friendship with Reema but had engaged in a pointless argument over a trivial topic. After submitting my designs, I felt overwhelmed by my loneliness, realizing that I hadn't changed at all and had exploded at Reema over something insignificant, just like before. I shared Reema's frightened reaction upon finding me on the floor and our enlightening conversation the following morning. I expressed the realization that I had been merely going through the motions of wanting to change because I thought it was the right thing to do, but I hadn't wholeheartedly embraced the change. I confided in Nandini about the need to release the fear, stop fixating on the past, and learn to move forward.

Nandini listened quietly, unsure of what to say. All she could do was lend an ear to my story and recognize why I appeared calmer and more at peace.

"I'm not sure what to say," she finally spoke, stepping closer and embracing me. "You've been through a lot, but it's evident that you've also learned a great deal."

I giggled, feeling a sense of relief. "Yes, I have indeed learned a lot about myself."

Nandini's next question held significance. "So, what do you plan on doing now? Would you like to continue our… so-called 'sessions'?"

I giggled again, appreciating the familiarity of our connection. "Yes, I definitely need our sessions. I don't think I'm ready to navigate everything on my own just yet. However, I feel a newfound confidence within myself now that I'm no longer living in fear. I've learned I shouldn't be afraid to share my feelings or struggles with you. I feel more assured in my abilities because, right now, I genuinely want to learn and grow."

"That's wonderful," Nandini responded, her voice calm and reassuring as we settled into our conversation. "I believe the best way for you to achieve that is by practicing the art of the highest choice. It's a thought exercise that involves consistently making the highest, most beneficial choice in any given situation."

Curiosity sparked within me as I listened intently. "Isn't that what we already do?" I asked, somewhat puzzled.

Nandini smiled gently. "It may seem that way, but let's delve deeper. Often, we tend to make choices based on our immediate emotions rather than taking a step back and engaging our rational minds. For example, a student might decide to hang out with friends instead of studying. At that moment, the student didn't pause to consider the potential consequences of their choice; they simply followed their feelings. Now, spending time with friends and taking breaks is important, but evaluating the situation and making the highest choice is essential."

She continued, gesturing toward our present interaction. "Even now, you have a choice. Should we engage in the art of the highest choice or not? It's up to you to consider your current circumstances and future aspirations and decide what truly constitutes the highest choice at this moment. Sometimes, a particular choice may bring immediate happiness, but upon closer examination, it may lead to an unfavorable future outcome. This concept even ties into the allure of instant gratification. People often prioritize short-term pleasure or results and end up making the wrong choices in the long run. Later, when faced with the consequences, it's often easier to shift blame onto others rather than accept responsibility. Our minds naturally work to protect us in such situations."

I realized the importance of developing mindful awareness when making decisions, considering their long-term implications rather than solely seeking instant gratification. Reflecting on my past choices, I recognized how I often resorted to alcohol as a coping mechanism, seeking temporary relief without considering the long-term consequences. Many of my negative choices were impulsive, without considering the future ramifications. If I had taken a moment to pause and ask myself, "What is the best choice in this situation?" I might have avoided those mistakes. For instance, I wouldn't have lashed out at Reema the other day if I had stopped to think, "What is the highest choice here? Is this argument worth jeopardizing our friendship? How will it impact both of us in the long run?" Even a brief consideration of the future would have helped me control my anger and handle the situation more effectively, sparing both of us the heartache.

"How can I determine the highest choice when there are numerous possibilities?"

"The highest choice is determined by your conscience, the inner voice that serves as an internal compass that guides us all. Have you ever found yourself in a situation where you knew something was wrong, and it made you feel uncomfortable?"

"Yes, particularly when I was younger. I recall when my friend pleaded with me to let her cheat on my exam. Deep down, I didn't want to comply, but eventually, I gave in because I didn't want my friend to dislike me."

"That discomfort you experienced reflects your moral compass at work. As a child, it wasn't easy to consider a wide range of options and identify the highest choice. It may have seemed like you had only two choices—to cheat or not to cheat. However, the concept of the highest choice reveals that there are often more possibilities to explore. For instance, you could have offered to help your friend study instead of resorting to cheating. There are always multiple alternatives, but the discomfort you feel arises due to the internal conflict between your conscience and actions. Some may ignore their conscience and prioritize friendship over integrity, while others will heed their conscience and prioritize integrity over friendship."

"I understand. It's like when I was aware that drinking was wrong, but I still chose to do it, and it made me feel uncomfortable."

"Exactly. At that moment, you acted based on your emotions. You didn't want to feel left out, so you gave in and went against your conscience. If you had taken a moment to pause and reflect on the potential consequences, you might have decided not to start drinking. This would have prevented you from making excuses to justify going against your conscience."

As Nandini prepared a snack, I opened my journal and reflected on our discussion.

Cultivating mindful awareness is crucial when making decisions, allowing us to consider their long-term implications instead of succumbing to instant gratification. By examining our past choices, we gain insight into patterns of behavior that may not align with our values. Pausing to evaluate the highest choice in a given situation helps us avoid impulsive actions and potential regrets. The discomfort we feel when we act against our conscience serves as a valuable signal from our moral compass. Embracing the concept of the highest choice empowers us to explore alternative options and make decisions that uphold our values and principles. Through this process, we nurture greater self-awareness and make choices that lead to personal growth and positive outcomes.

Returning with her homemade chickpea cutlets, Nandini and I spent the day chatting. Connecting with her as a friend and guide was refreshing rather than just a teacher. I felt a newfound comfort in our conversations, knowing I could speak openly without fear of offense. We delved into discussions about the upcoming Mumbai Fashion Trade Show, and I hoped that one day, my designs would grace such a prominent platform.

15

Beyond the Whys, Embracing the Hows

A week later, Nandini delivered the unfortunate news to me, "Sorry, Eshu, your designs were not selected. But they are ready to give you one more chance at my request."

The weight of disappointment settled upon me like a heavy cloak, enveloping me in a cloud of self-doubt. My heart sank, and a whirlwind of emotions consumed my thoughts. How could this have happened? I had poured my heart and soul into those designs, meticulously crafting each detail with unwavering dedication. Could it be that this downfall in my life has stunted my creativity?

As Nandini relayed the news, I couldn't help but question myself. Doubt crept in, undermining my confidence. I wondered whether my recent personal conflict with Reema had affected my work. Did that argument hinder my ability to channel my creativity? Was I unable to give my designs the attention and focus they deserved? The weight of self-criticism bore down on me, threatening to shatter my belief in my abilities. The nagging voice in my head whispered, "Maybe you're just not good enough." I felt the sting of tears behind my eyes, fighting to break free.

"Calm down; they rejected your designs because they were too elaborate and complex."

I countered, "Too elaborate and complex? Isn't it a good thing? All of my best designs have been the most elaborate and complex."

Nandini explained, "You are used to designing for the ramp, but remember this is for customers who come to stores. Normal people do not generally buy more complex dresses. You have to keep the clientele first."

Seeing my shocked expression, Nandini reached out, her comforting words like a lifeline. She reminded me of our acceptance mantra, the philosophy we had embraced together. "Not all is lost," she reassured me gently.

I found myself sitting quietly, trying to calm my racing thoughts. As I took deep breaths, a sense of rationality slowly returned. I reminded myself of the acceptance mantra I had embraced and gradually began to accept what had happened.

A flurry of questions filled my mind. Should I reach out to old co-workers and ask for referrals? Could I contact previous contractors I've worked with to explore potential job opportunities? Why hadn't I considered the preferences of the clientele beforehand? I knew this job was different from what I was used to, and I should have accounted for that.

However, Nandini's reassuring voice cut through my tangled thoughts. "Please don't worry too much," she said. "I have already requested another chance for you, and they are willing to review another submission. So please calm down, and let's think of where to go from here. It is important to shift your focus from the 'whys' to the 'hows.'"

I understood that dwelling on past actions and questioning my decisions incessantly would only impede my progress. Instead, I needed to channel my energy into constructive thinking and finding solutions.

Nandini continued, "When faced with disappointment or setbacks, pondering what went wrong and seeking answers is natural. Yet, fixating on the past and endlessly ruminating in self-doubt rarely yields positive outcomes. To truly move forward and continue growing, you must consciously shift your perspective to the 'how.' 'How can I improve my next design? How can I overcome this challenge?' By focusing on these questions, you would direct your attention toward seeking opportunities for improvement rather than getting trapped in past regrets."

After some contemplation, I realized that by letting go of the "whys," I would release myself from the shackles of self-doubt and regret. It was time to liberate my creative energies, allowing them to flow freely and fuel my determination to excel. This shift in mindset would empower me to learn from past experiences, viewing setbacks as valuable lessons that would transform and shape my future endeavors.

As Nandini shared her insights, she explained the distinct expectations and requirements of designing for a boutique instead of the ramp that I am used to. I started to understand that the boutique had its unique style, a different aesthetic that needed to be catered to. This realization fueled my resolve to delve deeper into my craft, explore new possibilities, and challenge myself to push beyond my comfort zone.

With renewed purpose, we sat down in her work studio. I immersed myself in extensive market research, studying the latest fashion trends, analyzing customer preferences, and studying the boutique's target audience. Armed with this knowledge, I embarked on remaking my designs.

Every stroke of the pencil became an opportunity to pour my emotions onto the paper, infusing my creations with a newfound depth. I experimented with different fabrics, textures, and colors, meticulously fine-tuning each element to bring my vision to life. It was a labor of love, a testament to my unwavering passion for fashion. I could feel the creative juices flow. I no longer felt stuck. Compared to the first time I submitted the designs, I was no longer designing for the sake of the job; I was designing again for the love of fashion.

Days turned into nights as I tirelessly worked, my determination unyielding. The setbacks I had faced became stepping stones, propelling me forward rather than holding me back. I embraced my mistakes, using them as invaluable lessons to refine and perfect my designs. During this time Reema and I had started talking again. Both Reema and Nandini were giving me valuable feedback.

As I submitted my designs, I felt a sense of accomplishment. Regardless of the outcome, I knew I had already defied the doubts that once plagued me. I had transformed adversity into an opportunity. And I once again fell in love with fashion.

16

Rising Above Past Missteps

A week later, Nandini invited me to her place. I could sense a contagious excitement in the air as I stepped into her room. Without containing her enthusiasm, Nandini burst into the room with a bright smile, her eyes shining. As she spoke, her words filled my heart with joy and relief, just like a schoolgirl waiting with anticipation when her annual exam results are announced.

"Esha, guess what? You won't believe it! Your designs have been selected!" Nandini exclaimed, her voice brimming with excitement.

A rush of emotions engulfed me - a mixture of elation, disbelief, and nervous anticipation. I felt a wave of pride welling up inside me, knowing that my hard work and dedication had paid off. The opportunity I had been eagerly waiting for was finally within reach.

A wide smile spread across my face as I replied, "Oh my goodness, Nandini! That's incredible news! I can't believe it!"

Nandini's smile grew wider as she continued, "And that's not all! They have scheduled an interview for you tomorrow. This is your chance to shine, Esha!"

My heart skipped a beat at the thought of the interview. While excitement coursed through my veins, a twinge of nervousness also took hold. It was a crucial moment that could shape my future in the industry, and I was determined to make the most of it.

Taking a deep breath to steady my nerves, I responded, "Thank you so much for believing in me, Nandini. I am both thrilled and nervous about the interview. It's an incredible opportunity, and I won't let it slip through my fingers."

Nandini clasped her hands together and offered words of encouragement, "Esha, you are talented and deserve this chance. Just be yourself, showcase your passion, and let your creativity shine. I have complete faith in you."

Her unwavering support brought a sense of reassurance and confidence. I realized that I am not alone in this journey. With Nandini by my side, I felt renewed determination and resolve.

As we discussed the upcoming interview, Nandini shared some valuable insights and tips based on her own experiences. Her guidance proved to be invaluable, helping me gain a clearer understanding of what to expect and how to present myself in the best possible light.

Grateful for her advice, I expressed my heartfelt appreciation, "Nandini, I can't thank you enough for all your support and guidance. Your belief in me means the world. I promise to make the most of this opportunity and show them what I am capable of."

Nandini smiled warmly, her eyes filled with pride. "Esha, it's your time to shine. I know you will do great things. Now, let's prepare for tomorrow's interview and make sure you leave a lasting impression!"

The next day arrived, and I found myself standing nervously in front of Ms. Nina Agarwal, the esteemed owner of Impression Designs. She exuded an air of confidence and elegance, dressed impeccably in her late forties.

"Hello, Ms. How are you today?" I greeted her, reaching out my arm, attempting to conceal my nerves.

"Hello, Ms. Esha. I'm doing well, thank you!" She replied with a composed demeanor and took my hand in hers to shake it.

With a warm smile, she gestured for me to take a seat. "Sure, have a seat, Esha. Nandini and I are familiar with each other. She has briefed me about you," Ms. Agarwal said, putting me at ease.

I couldn't help but wonder what Nandini had shared about my journey and past struggles. However, Ms. Agarwal swiftly changed the subject, reassuring me, "But let's move forward."

Relieved, I nodded in agreement, grateful to shift the focus to the present moment.

"I was impressed by your redesigns, and we are looking for someone to help us expand our formal Indo-Western wear. Do you have experience with that?" Ms. Agarwal inquired, her eyes displaying genuine interest.

"I have extensive experience with formal wear, but to be honest, I haven't specifically worked with Indo-Western wear. However, I have a true passion for the sector and often incorporate it into my personal style. I also have significant research experience, and I believe I can adapt quickly," I responded, feeling a surge of confidence.

She continued, explaining another role they were seeking to fill. "We also need an in-house stylist who can assist our special clients in selecting items for their wardrobe tailored to their body, style, and occasion. Have you done personal styling before?"

My heart skipped a beat. "No, I haven't had the opportunity to delve into personal styling before," I admitted, hoping it wouldn't be a setback.

Undeterred, Ms. Agarwal leaned forward and asked with a hint of excitement, "Are you ready to learn?"

A surge of enthusiasm rose within me, and I answered with determination, "Yes! I am eager to learn and embrace this new opportunity."

Ms. Agarwal proceeded to elaborate on the importance of client interaction and the unique experience they aimed to provide. "You will work closely with clients, attending to their personal preferences and dislikes. We want to offer an experience that goes beyond mere shopping, where everything is uniquely personalized and customized, crafted to help them discover and define their unique style. Can you do that?" she asked, her gaze unwavering.

Feeling invigorated, I responded confidently, "Certainly! It will be a new venture, and I'm excited to develop this skill. I welcome the opportunity to create a truly tailored experience for our clients."

"I appreciate your enthusiasm and passion. However, it is of utmost importance to address the matter of your past. As part of our standard procedure, we conduct comprehensive background checks on all prospective hires, and I am fully informed about the results we have obtained. Nonetheless, I must acknowledge that Nandini has spoken quite favorably about you, which has piqued my interest. I believe that personal growth and change are indeed possible for all people. All I truly want to know is if you are ready for the responsibilities that come with this role."

I paused for a moment, reflecting on my journey and the lessons I had learned. With conviction in my voice, I assured her, "Yes, ma'am. I understand that my career may not be at its peak right now, but if given a chance, I will wholeheartedly dedicate myself to this opportunity. I am committed to delivering my best."

Ms. Agarwal leaned back in her chair, a sense of satisfaction evident on her face. "Alright then, you are hired. You can meet the HR team; they will handle all the necessary details. You will work closely with Mr. Sanjay Bhatt, our Chief Designer and Store Manager. My assistant, Suhani, will introduce you. Good luck!"

I felt a wave of relief as Ms. Agarwal confirmed my employment. A sense of gratitude and excitement swelled within me, knowing I had been given a chance to prove myself in this new chapter of my career.

"Thank you so much, ma'am. I truly appreciate this opportunity," I expressed sincerely, a broad smile spreading across my face.

Ms. Agarwal reciprocated the smile, her eyes gleaming with confidence. "You're welcome, Esha. I believe in giving people a chance to grow and showcase their potential. I see your determination, and I'm confident you will contribute greatly to our team."

With a final nod, Ms. Agrawal signaled the conclusion of our meeting. Feeling a mix of elation and eagerness, I rose from my seat, ready to embark on this new professional endeavor.

As I made my way out of Ms. Agarwal's office, Suhani, her assistant, approached me with a warm and welcoming smile. "Congratulations, Esha! I've heard wonderful things about your work and am excited to have you join the team. Allow me to show you around and introduce you to your colleagues."

Grateful for her kind words and guidance, I followed Suhani as she led me through the vibrant office space. Each step brought me closer to a future filled with creative opportunities, personal growth, and the chance to leave behind my past mistakes.

With every interaction and introduction, I was met with warm greetings and genuine enthusiasm from my new colleagues. It was evident that the team at Impression Designs fostered a supportive and collaborative environment, which only amplified my excitement for what lay ahead.

After meeting all my new colleagues, I left the office with a light heart. I stood in front of the store for a while, taking it all in. This is the place I will be working from now on. It was a beautiful and elegant boutique with five floors, and the top floor was dedicated to office purposes.

Upon arriving home, I immediately called Nandini to share the wonderful news. Her genuine happiness for me was evident as she wished me luck. Recognizing that Nandini was the catalyst behind this second opportunity, I firmly committed to giving it my utmost effort. I was profoundly grateful for this chance and eagerly anticipated reintegrating into the working world.

Proceeding to the kitchen, I prepared a delightful meal for Reema and myself. When she arrived home, we enjoyed a pleasant dinner while exchanging stories about our respective days. The comforting thought of sharing a delightful meal with Reema brought me joy. It's a heartwarming notion representing the essence of a contented life— to have a fulfilling job and someone at home with whom to converse. I cherished the sense of stability that was now settling into my life.

17

Quest for Creative Fulfillment

As days turned into weeks and weeks transformed into a month, I once again sought solace in Nandini's presence.

"How is it going, Eshu? How has your first month at Impression been?" Nandini inquired.

I hesitated a little. I had been enjoying it yet also struggling. How should I describe this? "It's a little complicated. It's demanding and hectic, but it's a welcome change from sitting at home! It feels like my brain is finally being put back to use. It's a good kind of tiring work," I replied, "but sometimes I find myself feeling lost. I'm grateful that everything is finally settling down, but there are moments when I question if I'm truly doing the right thing," I admitted.

"What do you mean by doing the right thing?" Nandini inquired.

"I just mean, is this what I am meant to do? I know I have always wanted to work in fashion, but after everything I have gone through in this industry, maybe it happens for a reason. Like maybe I was meant to work here?"

With a gentle smile, Nandini offered her guidance, which I had grown more receptive to now. She suggested, "To generate clarity about your aim, try expressing it in the following format:"

"I am (Part 1)_____ who (Part 2)_____ so that (Part 3)_____."

She explained the significance of Part 1, "by stating 'I am' instead of 'I will be,' the mind can be influenced to believe in the achievement of the desired role. This alignment of thoughts, actions, and reactions paves the way for turning the envisioned future into reality. Part 2, captures the essence of how the chosen role is put into action, while Part 3 emphasizes the profound impact these actions have on others and humanity as a whole.

"Crafting Part 1 and Part 2 is relatively straightforward. You simply express who you are and what you do. However, Part 3 demands contemplation. It is often referred to as the 'Impersonal goal' because selecting an impersonal goal directs individuals towards a path of peace rather than personal struggles."

"Why should ambition be impersonal?" I inquired.

"An excellent question. Let's consider the example of someone whose sole aspiration is making money. Such an individual may encounter numerous obstacles that leave them feeling trapped and unfulfilled. Suppose they are waiting for a promotion that never happens; they might begin to doubt their worthiness for the job because their goal revolves solely around personal financial gain. However, if their mission were more impersonal, such as 'advocating financial freedom for all,' they would be better equipped to navigate such challenges. An impersonal mission extends far beyond the limited demands of their individual identity. Hence, all their personal interests appear minuscule in comparison when they are driven by an impersonal goal. Whenever they question their purpose, they can explore alternative avenues to attain that promotion while advancing the cause of financial freedom.

"I see. I believe I can answer Part 1 and Part 2, but I'm unsure about my mission in life."

"That's entirely normal. Deciding something as significant as your life's mission takes time. By being able to answer Part 1, you already possess a clear sense of identity. If you can respond to Part 2, it signifies that you understand your role in finding fulfillment. When you can address Part 3, you will have discovered your life mission and will strive to fulfill it.

"By emphasizing Part 1 ('I am'), one may decide to become a teacher, achieving their personal vision. By focusing on Part 2, they gain a deeper understanding of their role within their mission. For instance, if their sentence is 'I am a teacher who teaches young children...,' their Part 2 would be teaching, which provides clarity about what they are meant to do. Now, let's extend that with Part 3, an impersonal mission: 'I am a teacher who teaches young children, to nurture the minds of the next generation so that they grow to be magnanimous beings with higher values to serve society selflessly.' This formulation grants the teacher a clear mission. Suppose the teacher encounters difficulties and can no longer teach. If they only have Part 1 and Part 2, they may feel lost, thinking they can no longer fulfill their purpose. However, if they also have Part 3, which is more important for them than Part 1 and Part 2, they will understand that all is not lost; they can still tutor kids or write textbooks to contribute to their mission in life.

"The key lies in emphasizing the third part. Outstanding leaders distinguish themselves by their focus on Part 3. When your genuine focus revolves around Part 3 (so that _____), it signifies an impersonal vision. It reminds you of your contribution to society as a whole, highlighting the impact your presence can have in this world. While Parts 1 and 2 can keep you motivated on the path toward your desired position, it is Part 3 that sustains you through all obstacles. It fuels your passion, as there are many ways to achieve your mission."

Reflecting on her words, I synthesized my understanding. "Therefore, I can confidently state, 'I am a fashion designer who creates garments that reflect people's personalities, ensuring their comfort while keeping them stylish and trendy so that they feel comfortable and confident at times when it really matters to them.'"

Nandini nodded with an approving smile. "Precisely! Your statement is clear and concise and offers a strong foundation to refer back to when you encounter any uncertainties regarding your purpose.

"Now, let's analyze what you've expressed. Your identity is encapsulated in 'I am a fashion designer,' while your actions revolve around 'creating garments for people.' Lastly, your mission encompasses designing clothes that project individuals' personalities, prioritize their comfort, and exude a sense of smart and trendy fashion so that they feel confident and comfortable. By framing it this way, you open up multiple pathways to achieve your mission. Whether you work in high fashion or everyday wear, you can still fulfill your purpose.

"Part 3 of what you just stated means that your mission is to build a sense of comfort and confidence in your clients. So, you may even go the extra mile beyond fashion design to help them achieve this. You can redefine your Part 2 in ways that enable your clients to develop a more confident self-image beyond the remits of fashion!"

"That's absolutely true. Even before I entered this industry, my sole desire was to pursue fashion because I loved to study what made people feel more confident in their personalities. The sector itself was secondary. As you pointed out, regardless of my previous job or current one, I can still realize my mission."

"Pay attention to the principles and values you intend to uphold, how you will embody them, your deepest intentions, and the reasons behind your chosen path. This strengthens your confidence, as your established principles lend fortitude to your thoughts and enhance your willpower.

"How are things in other aspects of work? Are there any other concerns or issues you're facing? And how is your relationship with your colleagues?" Nandini probed, her genuine concern evident in her voice.

"Actually, something else has been weighing on my mind," I confessed. "During team meetings regarding personal styling, Sanjay, my boss, tends to favor Maya's opinion over mine. It's disheartening and makes me feel undervalued. I have valuable ideas, but they don't seem to consider them."

Attentive to my words, Nandini inquired, "Why do you think Sanjay behaves that way?"

"Perhaps he prefers Maya's work over mine. Although she doesn't have any formal expertise in evening wear, she aspires to move into that area and has been handling those clients temporarily until I was brought in for the position," I explained, frustration evident in my voice.

"So, you believe she has vested interests in securing your position?"

"I am not sure. While Maya seeks my opinions on certain designs and supports me, it seems there's a shift when it comes to a particular client order, and Sanjay tends to favor her. However, I have more experience and have worked with bigger clients."

Nandini interrupted my self-criticism, "It's understandable that these circumstances can leave you feeling negative and discouraged. But stop putting yourself down. Remember our mantra and practice acceptance," she encouraged.

"Yes, you're right. That mantra has helped me keep going. In fact, I've been trying to accept the 'non-acceptance' in this situation," I admitted.

"Great. You're doing well!" Nandini commended.

"Now, let's approach the situation with a more objective lens. Does Sanjay always prefer Maya's opinion?" Nandini prompted.

As I delved into my thoughts, I realized it wasn't a consistent pattern. "No, not always. He generally considers everyone's opinions, but there are certain cases where it seems he gives more weight to Maya's input," I shared with Nandini.

"Good. Now, let's go deeper. Since we don't have the complete picture, Sanjay's preference for Maya's opinion may stem from specific clients or projects. Some clients may have specific demands or unique preferences, and Maya, having worked with them before you joined, may better understand their tastes. In those cases, Sanjay might value her insights more as your designs would cater more to generalized requests rather than their personal tastes," Nandini suggested.

As I pondered Nandini's words, a sense of clarity emerged. It all seemed logical, and I began to understand the possible reasons behind the dynamics at play.

"Let me share a personal example to clarify this point. Remember how we used to watch movies together when we were younger?" Nandini reminisced.

"Of course! That's where our love for fashion began!" I replied with a hint of nostalgia.

"Well, during my college years, I joined an aspiring filmmakers club and often faced similar situations. I felt that the group favored other members' ideas over mine. But when I took a step back and looked at the overall picture, I realized there was nothing inherently wrong with it," she explained.

"Even though they preferred other people's ideas, if they truly valued your ideas, why not combine them?" I inquired, seeking further clarification.

"That was my initial thought as well," she replied, "but then I realized that it's actually a good thing. In a creative process, it's natural for some ideas to be rejected. If every idea were to be combined, the end product might become muddled due to conflicting concepts. Sometimes certain ideas are chosen while others are not, and that's part of the creative journey. After all, isn't the purpose of meetings to find the best outcome for a given scenario? Although it can be discouraging when your idea isn't chosen, if we view our teammates as contributors on our life's journey, we can shift from competition to learning from one another."

I nodded, understanding the perspective. "At the end of the day, it's the final product that matters to the customer. Even if they choose my design, if it doesn't resonate with their taste, all the effort would go to waste," I added, emphasizing the importance of considering the customer's needs.

"Consider the people around you as partners, contributors, or co-creators in your life's journey," Nandini continued. "Those who provoke negative feelings within you are actually providing you an opportunity for growth and compassion. They may play a negative role in your life, but ultimately, they are your co-creators."

Reflecting on Nandini's words, I felt a sense of guilt. People who had played negative roles in my life might have inadvertently taught me valuable lessons. It reminded me of a conversation I had with Reema, where I realized how a toxic relationship had ultimately helped her learn important lessons while I was blinded by my emotions.

"That's true," I acknowledged. "Everyone is a co-creator in our lives, and even those who provoke negative feelings within us might be helping us or preparing us in some way as Reema did with the arguments we had."

"Exactly, but sometimes, we fail to see that. When people don't respond as we want them to, it's important to accept the situation and try to practice forgiveness and understanding from their perspective. When we put ourselves in their shoes, we can better understand their decisions. It's crucial to welcome diverse perspectives and work toward a common vision. Having a variety of viewpoints is a strength that can lead to collective progress in a shared direction."

"I usually try to avoid conflict because I dislike being disliked, so I often incorporate everyone's ideas to please everyone," I admitted.

"Learning to navigate conflicts creatively is a skill worth developing," Nandini affirmed. "The belief that conflict is inherently negative is often limiting. Conflict can actually lead to innovative solutions and personal growth. Embracing diverse perspectives allows us to broaden our ideas and create something unique."

"I do enjoy brainstorming with Sanjay at times," I shared, recalling a recent incident where we had different opinions about a design. "It sparks more creativity and understanding."

"That's great to hear! To stay focused and appreciate your progress, try this practice: Take five minutes before starting your work to plan your day and five minutes at the end to review your entire day. Write down the activities you've accomplished, the pending tasks, and any obstacles you've encountered. When you can see your accomplishments for the day, it becomes difficult to doubt yourself," Nandini suggested.

"I see. That sounds like a helpful suggestion. It's similar to my journaling practice, and I'll definitely try it," I responded, giving Nandini a thumbs-up.

We spent the rest of the day chatting and watching some of the short videos Nandini had worked on during her college years. It was enjoyable to see the final products that her group had created, despite differences in opinions and ideas. It reminded me once again that collaboration and embracing diverse perspectives could lead to remarkable outcomes.

As the next week started and I began to observe my interactions with Maya and Sanjay closely, I found that Nandini was right; they had no intentions of putting me down but, in fact, were taking their trusted clients into consideration.

Looking at this from a new perspective, my entire story about them ignoring me and trying to put me down seemed silly and crazy. I felt a sense of lightness as I let go of my unnecessary negative beliefs.

18

Tempted by the Allure

On a rainy afternoon, I was engrossed in a new movie, seeking comfort in the world of cinema. The characters on the screen were celebrating a Christian wedding with a heartfelt toast, raising their glasses. As I watched the scene unfold, conflicting emotions stirred within me. I couldn't help but wonder how people could use alcohol to celebrate joyous occasions when it had brought me so much pain. However, as I continued watching, I felt a familiar longing, a craving for something I had been trying hard to leave behind.

Amidst my internal struggle, I remembered a bottle I had found while cleaning, tucked away in the depths of my cupboard. It was a costly bottle given to me by my coworkers after my first big promotion, and I had been saving it for a special occasion. But something strange happened. Even amidst the frustration building within me, I couldn't resist the allure of the sweet wine. With a surge of desperation, I retrieved the bottle. Holding it in my hands, I was flooded with suppressed sensations and memories I had fought so hard to resist.

I gave in to temptation and took a hesitant sip. The taste, the sensation—it was like rekindling a long-lost flame, a forbidden pleasure that still had its allure. At that moment, I questioned why I had chosen to forsake this temporary escape from the harsh realities of life.

As the liquid coursed through my veins, I felt a fleeting euphoria enveloping me. It was as if I were weightless, suspended in mid-air, floating among the clouds. I felt on top of the world, but just as quickly, I imagined myself plummeting from a rooftop. A memory I had suppressed for so long rushed to the forefront of my mind—the memory of a cloudy night on a rooftop when I had contemplated giving it all up.

My body instinctively reacted to purge the poison that threatened to consume me. I stumbled to the restroom, praying that expelling the liquid from my system would somehow cleanse my soul. Nausea churned within me as I desperately tried to rid myself of the intoxicating venom.

Kneeling on the cold bathroom floor, tears mingled with regret, guilt, and shame. How could I have succumbed so easily? I felt like a failure, trapped by my weaknesses. The weight of my transgression pressed upon me, threatening to crush my spirit.

In my darkest hour, I wanted to reach out to someone for solace, anyone. With a trembling hand, I dialed Nandini's number and recounted the events that had unfolded. There was a comforting pause as she listened, allowing me to gather myself to find a semblance of calm amidst the storm raging within.

When Nandini finally spoke, her voice carried the wisdom and empathy of a dear friend who understood the struggles of my journey. She reminded me that this setback was not the end and that setbacks were a natural part of the recovery process. Her words soothed my wounded spirit, infusing me with a glimmer of hope that had seemed distant, moments ago.

Sitting on the bathroom floor, I clung to her words, letting the tears flow freely as if each droplet symbolized release and renewal. Time stretched before me, offering a blank canvas on which I could paint a different tomorrow.

With a resolve strengthened by adversity, I remained on the bathroom floor a little longer, allowing my emotions to settle and finding the strength to face the challenges ahead. The cool tiles against my skin grounded me, reminding me of my inner strength, even in moments of weakness.

I attempted to stand up, but my legs gave out. After a few more tries, I managed to stand and took hesitant steps toward the mirror. I wiped away my tears and washed my face, trying to regain composure. I closed my eyes and recited the acceptance mantra, allowing myself to calm my fast-beating heart. What now? I had thought I had overcome my addiction since I no longer craved it every day, but it was a different story when faced with it directly. I slapped my cheeks gently, taking a deep breath. Okay, it's time to move past this. What happened had happened. All I could do was learn from it and keep moving forward.

Leaving the sanctuary of the restroom behind, I embraced the challenges that awaited me. Each step I took resonated with resilience, a testament to my unwavering determination to overcome the allure of addiction. I knew it wouldn't be easy, but I was ready to confront my weaknesses head-on.

As I made another phone call to Nandini, the anticipation of meeting with her swirled inside me. We had planned to get together at her house, and as I arrived at her doorstep, she greeted me with open arms and a warm hug. "Oh, Esha, you've had quite a day," she exclaimed, her voice filled with empathy. "But it's going to be okay. I know it's hard, but trust me, everything will work out."

A giggle escaped my lips, the first genuine one I had experienced all day. Deep down, I knew the words she spoke, but hearing them from her brought a soothing comfort. "Thank you, Nandu," I replied gratefully. "I know things will get better with time, but I'm struggling to make sense of it all right now."

Nandini joined in the laughter, a shared moment of lightness amidst the heaviness of my emotions. Leading me into her cozy living room, she shared her wisdom. "Sweet things always help when we're feeling down," she said, handing me a steaming mug of tea and a plate piled high with freshly baked cookies.

As the warmth of the tea enveloped me, and the scent of the cookies filled the air, a sense of tranquility settled over me. It was a realization that I had been missing—an understanding that having someone beside me to share the weight of my emotions made a world of difference.

"Okay, let's talk about what you mentioned earlier," Nandini began, settling into a chair opposite me. "You mentioned that you're unsure how to process everything in the present."

I nodded, sipping the comforting tea. "Yes, exactly. I keep telling myself that in time, I'll be fine. But I'm struggling to find effective ways to cope with it all right now."

Nandini leaned forward, her eyes sparkling with wisdom. "I understand. Coping mechanisms are like mental exercises that help us navigate difficult experiences and move forward. Personally, I find solace in self-talk."

"Self-talk?" I questioned, curiosity dancing in my eyes. "You mean talking to oneself? Isn't that something we all do?"

Nandini nodded, a gentle smile gracing her face. "Indeed, it is. Self-talk is the internal dialogue within our minds—the continuous flow of thoughts, beliefs, and interpretations that we use to communicate with ourselves. It can be positive, negative, or neutral, shaping our emotions, behaviors, and overall well-being."

The idea intrigued me, and I leaned in, eager to grasp its essence. "So, positive self-talk means thinking positively, while negative self-talk means the opposite?"

Nandini's eyes lit up as she delved deeper into the concept. "Precisely. Self-talk plays a pivotal role in our cognition and can greatly influence our emotions and actions. Becoming aware of our self-talk patterns and consciously cultivating positive and supportive self-talk can lead to personal growth, resilience, and achieving our goals. When we affirm to ourselves, 'I am capable of achieving my goals with hard work and perseverance,' it boosts our self-confidence and motivation. We begin to believe in our abilities, take action, and witness increased productivity and a higher likelihood of success."

Her words resonated deeply, and I couldn't help but nod in agreement. "But what about negative self-talk?" I asked, my voice tinged with curiosity.

Nandini's expression softened, her tone filled with kindness. "Negative self-talk can be detrimental. When our minds fill with thoughts like 'I always mess things up. I'm such a failure. I don't deserve it,' it chips away at our self-esteem, engendering feelings of worthlessness and dampening our motivation to face challenges or pursue our goals. It reinforces negative beliefs about ourselves, leading to a sense of helplessness. However, there is also neutral self-talk, which is more objective and factual. It allows us to think or speak to ourselves in a descriptive manner without judgment or emotional bias. This self-talk is useful for problem-solving, decision-making, and organizing our thoughts. By adopting a neutral self-talk approach, we can focus on objective information, maintain emotional balance, and make effective decisions."

I absorbed her words, the revelation of the power of self-talk slowly sinking in. "I see," I murmured, contemplating the implications. "But if self-talk is something we already engage in, what difference does it make to know all this?"

Nandini's gaze held mine, her voice gentle yet firm. "You see, our minds often default to negative self-talk in challenging situations. And when we engage in such negativity, it accumulates within us, affecting not only our internal state but also our communication with others. However, by understanding the principles of positive self-talk and consciously practicing it, we can shape our mental world. We can take charge of our thoughts and guide our minds toward more positive paths. Our actions often contribute to our failures, but by steering our minds in the right direction through positive self-talk, we can overcome any obstacle."

A flicker of hope ignited within me, eager to learn more. "So, in my situation, where should I begin? Do I simply focus on positive thoughts?"

Nandini's eyes gleamed with wisdom as she imparted her guidance. "Indeed, focusing on positive thoughts is a great starting point. Additionally, you can employ positive affirmations to guide your life. For example, if you feel that you're surrounded by the wrong company, you can repeat an affirmation like 'I am always surrounded by people who are joyful, honest, and genuine, who aspire to live for an impersonal purpose.' By doing so, you create a mental filter that allows you to weed out those individuals who don't align with your criteria. Take some time to reflect on your life and what you truly desire. If you believe that 'I deserve a healthy and vibrant life' or 'I am healing and nurturing my body and mind,' you'll find it easier to resist temptations and make choices that honor your well-being. It may not happen overnight, but with consistent practice, you will gradually develop a strong belief in your self-worth, and your mind will follow suit. So, embrace the power of positive self-talk and let it guide you on your journey."

"I will definitely do that. To start with, I'll write some positive affirmations in my journal to help me use positive self-talk."

As the evening unfolded, Nandini and I continued our heartfelt conversation, delving into various aspects of positive self-talk and its transformative power. The hours slipped away unnoticed as we shared stories, insights, and laughter. It was an evening of connection and support, where the weight of my troubles felt lighter in the presence of a true friend.

As dusk turned into darkness, Nandini suggested we prepare dinner together. We gathered ingredients, chopped vegetables, and seasoned dishes with care. The aroma of spices filled the air, creating an ambiance of warmth and comfort. As we sat down to savor our homemade meal, our conversation shifted to dreams and aspirations and the power of positive self-talk to propel us toward our goals.

With the night winding down, I bid Nandini farewell and made my way home, a sense of hope and determination filling my heart. Inspired by our conversation, I resolved to start a notebook of positive affirmations—a collection of empowering words to guide me on my journey of self-discovery and growth. I knew that through positive self-talk, I could reshape my mindset, embrace my worth, and overcome any obstacle that came my way.

19

From Pressure to Pride

I stared at the invitation in my hand, my heart pounding with excitement and nervousness. It was an invitation to a prestigious Fashion Trade Show, followed by an after-party at one of the city's most popular nightclubs. A rush of memories flooded my mind as I recalled the first time I had set foot in that nightclub when I was new to Mumbai.

There, amidst the pulsating music and dazzling lights, I tasted alcohol for the first time. The experience had left a bitter taste in my mouth, and I had vowed never to drink it again. Little did I know back then that this promise would crumble quickly, turning into a regular habit and eventually transforming into an addiction that consumed me.

As I held the invitation, a conflicted mixture of anticipation and reluctance coursed through my veins. It had only been a few months since I broke my sobriety and had some alcohol. Since then, I had been constantly practicing self-talk, trying to rewire my thinking, and using 3D. I hadn't had a sip of alcohol since then.

Despite my reservations, my coworkers insisted that I join them for the show. Nandini saw it as an opportunity to face my inner demons and confront the challenges that lay before me. Reluctantly, I understood, realizing that it could serve as a test of my newfound strength and determination. In my favorite pink evening gown, I took a deep breath and stepped into one of the biggest fashion shows in the country.

Later that evening, the nightclub greeted me with its familiar atmosphere, dim lights casting an ethereal glow over the dancing crowd. But this time, for the first time in many months, I didn't feel the same eagerness that had once consumed me. Doubts gnawed at me, tempting me to turn back, to retreat to the safety of familiarity. "Come on, Esha," I whispered to myself, mustering the courage to continue forward. "Go in. No! What if I fail? What if I give in again? No, not this time. I am going to win. I am going to fight."

My inner struggle intensified with each step; a battle waged within the deepest recesses of my being. Persevering against the doubts that threatened to engulf me, I pressed on. As I approached my old friends sitting near the bar counter, a glimmer of dread washed over me. This was not what I needed—a circle of people to pressure me again.

With a fake smile, I greeted everyone, trying to mask the turmoil that churned within me. My eyes inadvertently flickered toward the wine glasses, and an all-too-familiar urge to reach for a mug of beer tugged at my senses. But this time, I swiftly reminded myself of 3D, of my commitment to delayed gratification. It was just an urge, a passing whisper of temptation.

Amidst the lively chatter and laughter, I couldn't help but question myself. "What exactly is happening?" I pondered, seeking the truth buried beneath the surface. "What is it that I truly want?" The answer reverberated through my mind, clear and unwavering. "I want to taste that drink. But who wants to taste it? Is it truly me, or just my mind? Is it my mind or merely the craving of my tongue?"

Determined to understand my desires, I chose to observe the feeling rather than succumb to it. And in that moment of focused introspection, the craving began to subside. A flicker of victory danced in my eyes as I confidently ordered a soft drink.

Ananya, seated on my right, gazed at me in awe. "What's wrong with you, Esha? Are you sick?" she exclaimed as she looked at the soda in my hand, genuine concern etched on her face. "Who orders that in a bar!? Come on... have a real drink," she insisted.

A mixture of determination and vulnerability colored my response. "No thanks, I'm good," I replied, the words carrying a weight that only I truly understood. Anisha, an ex-colleague who knew me well, interjected, "How can a soft drink be good? Don't worry, Esha, it's my treat." Diya, always one to join the conversation, chimed in, "Yeah, come on, girl! Just one drink! You can't let us down like that."

The pressure mounted, their words like a persistent drumbeat in my ears. But this time, I held my ground, unyielding in my resolution. "I don't want to; please don't force me," I pleaded, my voice tinged with vulnerability and strength. A palpable tension filled the air as my friends looked down, realizing the impact of their insistence.

Summoning every ounce of willpower, I pushed the drink away, distancing myself from the temptation that had once held me captive. I raised the soft drink to my lips and took a sip, the cool liquid a balm to my conflicted soul. Mixed emotions coursed through me—I felt a twinge of guilt for declining my friends' offers, yet internally, I was brimming with pride and empowerment. I had triumphed over the allure of immediate gratification, choosing instead the path of resilience.

Desiring to shift the focus away from my personal battle, I eagerly shared the news of submitting my designs for an important interview. It was a pivotal moment in my career, a glimmer of hope in a time of uncertainty. The conversation shifted, and my friends engaged fervently, discussing various topics and catching up on the latest news. My drinking habits, once the center of attention, now became a mere footnote in our lively exchange.

An unexpected revelation unfolded as Anisha uttered words that touched my heart. "Have you found a new job? I put in a word for you at Season's Fashion," she revealed, her eyes gleaming with genuine support. Gratitude welled up within me as I replied, "Oh wow, thank you so much. I have found a new job, and it's going great. Thank you for looking out for me." It was nice to hear that even when I felt no one was on my side, someone was thinking about my future. I guessed

I did not honestly think of them as my friends. I had assumed that they abandoned me when my life spiraled.

As the night progressed, the conversation delved into various topics, each word tinged with camaraderie and shared memories. Gossip and laughter intertwined, weaving a web of belonging and connection. Yet, as the hours ticked by, I felt a growing sense of contentment mingled with a newfound desire for solitude.

As the night ventured on, I realized it was getting late. I bid farewell to my friends and hugged them goodbye.

As I walked away from the pulsating energy of the nightclub, I called Nandini to share my triumph. Nandini listened with full attention, mirroring my joy and understanding. Her voice, filled with genuine pride and affection, resonated in my ears. "Esha, take a moment to reflect on everything that has transpired tonight," she advised. "Feel the weight of your achievement, for it is no small feat. You have not only resisted temptation but discovered the unwavering support of true friends. This is the power of delayed gratification—the ability to savor the pleasure of success and inner strength."

Although we planned to meet the next day, it was important for me to work through all my thoughts. I pulled out my journal and excitedly wrote down my accomplishments, connections, and all the amazing designs I saw today. I felt so motivated and inspired to design more.

"So, Eshu, how was yesterday? I can see that you're looking motivated. Come on, spill the beans," an equally enthusiastic Nandini asked the next day, curiosity dancing in her eyes.

"I didn't have a single sip of alcohol! I just drank a soda and chatted with old friends," I exclaimed, a sense of accomplishment swelling within me.

"Wow! Great!" Nandini exclaimed, unable to contain her excitement. She rose from her seat and enveloped me in a tight hug, her genuine pride and support palpable.

"I am so proud of you," she whispered, her voice filled with warmth and admiration. We settled back into our seats, our hands still entwined, a tangible connection between us.

"So, you've replaced 'hard drinks' with 'cold drinks.' Did this help you realize that the 'kick' you used to derive from drinks is actually not pleasurable?"

I nodded, my mind reeling with newfound insights. "It's true, Nandu. It actually works. But I still need more practice," I admitted, my voice tinged with determination and vulnerability.

"You will certainly encounter more situations where you'll be tested, but don't go around partying just to test yourself," Nandini teased, a playful glint in her eyes.

"No way, Nandu! I may be crazy, but not that crazy," I laughed, the sound echoing with a newfound lightness. I couldn't help but feel a rush of gratitude toward Nandini. "This is all due to you. I don't have enough words to thank you," I confessed, my voice filled with sincerity.

Nandini smiled, her eyes shining with a mixture of affection and understanding. "Thanks is due to the wisdom that I received from the retreat! I've been sharing whatever I understood from the discourses that I attended."

We continued our conversation, delving into various topics, our words laced with a sense of familiarity and comfort. As our conversation meandered, I couldn't help but share another revelation with Nandini.

"There's one more thing I wanted to share," I began, a hint of uncertainty creeping into my voice. "I actually didn't want to go to the party. I felt a little strange. I used to love attending such parties earlier, but this time, it was different. I thought I could utilize my time in a better way. I did go to the party and came back early. I could never have done this earlier. It's strange, but I'm feeling happy as well."

Nandini listened attentively, her eyes fixed on me, her presence unwavering. "That's a good start," she replied, her voice gentle yet filled with wisdom. "As you grow emotionally and spiritually, you'll realize that the actual aim in life is to experience pure love, lasting joy, and complete peace. You'll find yourself drawn to activities that bring higher contentment and fulfillment. Your choices will align with your true desires."

She continued, her words resonating deep within my soul. "Do you remember when we talked about making the highest choice? You need to put it into practice consciously. You thought through your options and what is best for you. You know partying was bad for you, but going to the trade show was a rare opportunity, so you made the best choices you could. Each and every choice that we make in life impacts us. Hence, we need to learn the art of consistently making the highest choice. The more you start implementing these small techniques into your daily life, the more you will learn to shape your life."

To make the highest choice consistently, I needed to decide what I wished to create in life and reiterate what I am aspiring towards.

We chatted for hours about all the newest designs of the season. As I made my way back, thoughts swirled within me, contemplating the lower choices I had made that had led me down the path of depression and instability. Yet, a newfound resolve ignited within me. "But now, I choose to be happy and make better choices in life for a brighter future. I also need to work on my personal finances," I affirmed, determination coloring my words.

20

A Birthday Call with Lingering Guilt

It was a warm summer day, and I found myself fixated on the calendar, a mix of anticipation and unease fluttering in my chest. This Friday marked my Dad's birthday, a special occasion we always celebrated, regardless of where I was. Even if I couldn't be there physically, we made sure to connect through video calls, sharing laughter and love across the miles. However, this year, something held me back.

I was overcome with a sense of fear at the thought of talking to my parents and pretending everything was fine when it wasn't. The truth was, I had never opened up to them about everything that had happened. Every time I considered reaching out, guilt consumed me, making it impossible to make that call, especially since that fateful night on the roof when my mind was clouded with thoughts of them.

Nandini, who was sitting by my side, sensed my distress. She looked at me with concern, her eyes filled with understanding. "Eshu," she said softly, her voice gentle. "You've been staring at your calendar for a while now. What's troubling you? Is everything alright?"

I took a deep breath and replied, "It's about my family. I'm terrified to talk to my parents. I carry so much guilt for my foolish actions in the past. My parents have always been there for me, granting me freedom and support. But I squandered that freedom, making a mess of my life. The guilt weighs heavily on me, and the only solace I find is using the acceptance mantra. Still, I'm afraid to reach out. They haven't reached out to me either. Sometimes, I worry they've given up on me."

Nandini's voice was gentle as she responded, her words offering comfort and reassurance. "Eshu, do you remember when we were young, and you told everyone you wanted to be a fashion designer? I remember all the neighbors warning you against it, saying a regular computer job would provide more opportunities and a stable source of income. But uncle and aunty never forced you to do anything or lectured you on what to do. They stood by your side, offering their unwavering support. Just like now, they are giving you space because they understand you. They know they can't fight your battles for you; all they can do is be there, ready to support you."

I knew deep down that Nandini was right. However, it felt easier to believe that my parents didn't care, allowing me to evade the guilt I carried. But I realized that I had let my own insecurities cloud my judgment.

In truth, my parents had always been there for me, supporting me in their own unique way. Even when I pushed them away, they continued to reach out, providing financial assistance, emotional support, and valuable advice. Looking back, I couldn't deny the love they had shown me. It was my own resistance and stubbornness that prevented me from appreciating it.

Acknowledging my mistakes and accepting my wrongdoings was a bitter pill to swallow. Blaming others seemed like an easier, less painful route. However, Nandini's words shattered that illusion, compelling me to face the truth. I couldn't ignore the fact that I had played a significant role in damaging our relationship.

Sensing my nervousness, Nandini offered a fresh perspective. "Balancing the five facets of life—social, emotional, physical, financial, and spiritual—is important," she said, her voice filled with wisdom. "Relationships with others are a vital part of life, and by isolating yourself, you deny yourself the joy and fulfillment that come from those connections."

Her words resonated deeply within me. I realized that by shutting myself off for fear of being hurt, I was also denying myself the happiness that genuine human connection brings. "That's true," I admitted, vulnerability seeping into my voice. "If I close myself off because I'm afraid of getting hurt, I'm also closing myself off from experiencing joy."

Nandini smiled warmly, her eyes sparkling. "Exactly, Eshu! Do you know why humans are called social creatures?" she asked gently.

Taking a moment to ponder, I ventured a guess. "Because we enjoy talking and interacting with others?"

Nandini chuckled softly. "In a way, yes," she replied. "It's because we need each other. Think back to when people lived in tribes. What were the chances of survival for someone on their own?"

Her question prompted me to reflect, and the truth behind her words became clear. "I would imagine the chances were quite low," I answered thoughtfully. "It would be challenging to handle everything—hunting, protecting territory, defending against predators—all alone."

"Exactly," Nandini nodded, understanding evident in her expression. "If we could survive independently, our ancestors wouldn't have needed to form tribes. Our need for social connection extends beyond mere emotional well-being. Throughout history, humans have relied on collaboration and cooperation to survive and thrive. Communication and coordination were essential for navigating the challenges of our environment."

As I listened, a profound understanding of our inherent social nature began to take shape. Nandini continued, sharing her knowledge. "Moreover, humans possess high emotional intelligence or EQ. While reptiles may be intelligent, they do not experience emotions as we do due to differences in brain structure. That's why domesticating reptiles is impossible. The complexity of human emotions is intricately tied to our brain structure and function."

Her words intrigued me, and I leaned closer, eager to learn more. "Unlike animals with simpler nervous systems, humans possess a highly developed limbic system, including the amygdala, hippocampus, and prefrontal cortex," she explained. "These brain regions are involved in processing and regulating emotions. They allow us to experience a wide range of emotions, from joy and love to fear and sadness, forming the foundation of our emotional intelligence."

Nandini's words struck a chord within me. I began to comprehend why controlling our emotions can be such a challenge. "That's why it's so difficult to control our emotions," I remarked, a mix of awe and frustration in my voice.

She nodded sympathetically. "Our emotions can be intense and overwhelming at times, making complete control elusive. This is partly due to the intricate interplay between our thoughts, emotions, and physiological responses. When confronted with certain triggers or situations, our emotions can quickly overpower our rational thinking, leading to impulsive or irrational behavior."

I couldn't help but agree, recalling moments when my own emotions had overwhelmed me. Nandini's insights shed light on the complexities of our human experience.

She continued, emphasizing the significance of our relationships. "Our connections with family, friends, and communities profoundly impact our emotional well-being and overall quality of life. Even in our modern society, social connections remain crucial for various aspects of our lives. Social networks provide opportunities for personal growth, career advancement, and social support. Meaningful relationships contribute to our mental and physical health, promoting resilience, happiness, and overall life satisfaction."

Nandini spoke gently, her eyes brimming with empathy. "You need to release the guilt, Esha," she said. "Positive energy and thoughts can profoundly influence your own sense of fulfillment. Let go of the past and open yourself to the possibilities of healing and growth."

"There is an intriguing story that revolves around the Indian word 'Tathastu,' meaning 'So be it.' Legend has it that the deities respond with 'So be it' when people make wishes. 'Let my family be happy' - 'Tathastu! So be it.' Or 'I am fed up with my family and all this relationship drama' - 'Tathastu! So be it.'"

She continued, "Whatever you focus on, grows in your life. It's like watering a plant. Imagine having a potted plant in your house. If you diligently water it, it flourishes and grows. However, if you neglect it, it withers away and eventually perishes. Or think about a part of your body, and you will start to feel it. For instance, if you think about your toe, it might start to feel heavy or hot because you are consciously choosing to think about it. Similarly, whatever you direct your attention towards, whether it's an object, a situation, a quality, or even people, they receive the energy of your attention and begin to thrive."

Nandini's words carried a profound wisdom. "Whether it's something you yearn for or something you wish to avoid," she continued, her voice filled with conviction, "the focus you lend to the qualities of others has a direct impact on how they unfold in your life. When you nurture and cherish the positive attributes of those around you, you create an environment for their growth and blossoming. On the flip side, if you fixate on the undesirable aspects of your relationships, they will gain prominence and influence. The concept of Tathastu goes beyond mere mythology; it is an active force that shapes our reality with every passing moment, guided by the thoughts we entertain." She paused for a moment and looked at me reassuringly, "So, even if fear still lingers within you when it comes to reaching out to your parents, if you simply think 'I will connect with my parents' and embrace that intention, your wish will be granted, and you will indeed make that call. The power of Tathastu will manifest your desire into reality."

I sat in silence, lost in my own thoughts. When did I let fear consume me, turning me into someone who believed everything I touched would turn negative? I know it wasn't true. I closed my eyes and thought, "I will call my parents and be honest with them, and whatever happens will happen."

With determination welling up, I resolved to confront my fears head-on. I refused to let fear control me any longer. It was time to mend the strained bonds with my parents, and I would do so by speaking from the heart. I embraced the uncertainty and accepted that whatever happened, I would face it with honesty and truth.

That Friday, after I came home from work, I reached for the phone, my hand trembling slightly. But in that tremor, I found a newfound strength—a defiance against the limitations I had imposed on myself. I took a deep breath and dialed Ma's number, feeling the weight of anticipation with every ring.

Finally, my mother's familiar voice broke the silence, filled with love and concern. At that moment, I realized that they had always loved me and were waiting for me to be ready. The walls of guilt and insecurity started to crumble, replaced by the understanding that our connection was still strong.

I had a heartwarming conversation with my parents over the phone, eagerly sharing the news of my new job and my delightful meeting with Nandini. Their voices filled with joy and pride, assuring me that I was on the right path and that they were happy for me. The familiar warmth in their words eased my worries, and I couldn't help but feel grateful for their unwavering support.

As we spoke, I mustered the courage to apologize to them, sincerely expressing my remorse for not being open about everything that had happened. The long-held burden of guilt seemed to dissipate as I poured out my heartfelt apology. I reassured them of my love and promised to make amends.

After the call ended, I sank into the softness of the couch, allowing tears to stream down my cheeks. It was an emotional release, a catharsis that left me feeling lighter and more at peace. The apology had been long overdue, but now that it was finally spoken, I sensed a renewed sense of hope and healing.

As the tears subsided, a newfound strength welled up within me. I made a firm promise to myself to visit my parents in a few months to celebrate Ayushi's birthday together and cherish the precious moments as a family. The prospect of reuniting filled me with anticipation and joy.

21

Stamping Out Judgment

The gentle sunlight streamed through the curtains, filling Nandu's cozy living room with a warm glow. I sat across her, savoring a cup of tea as we engaged in a deep conversation about the pleasant interaction I had with my family. Nandini shared in my joy.

A question arose in my mind, a topic we had touched upon in our previous discussions. "Do you remember when we talked about how our focus shapes our experiences, using the example of plants? What happens when a negative thought lingers in my mind, like someone being rude to me, and I can't help but give it attention? It has turned my mind into a toxic place, and I'm not sure why I do that."

Nandini gladly explained, "Every aspect of our life is influenced by the relationships we have with ourselves and the beliefs we've developed throughout our journey. The world is a profound mirror, reflecting our inner state. Our external experiences often intertwine with our self-talk and internal dynamics, ultimately impacting the world around us."

Intrigued by this interconnectedness, I interjected, "So, when someone is rude to me, it means that I am rude to others. If others take me for granted, does it mean that I am taking them for granted?"

Nandini smiled, "No. It doesn't necessarily mean we are rude to others. But it could suggest that we may be harboring rudeness within ourselves. Perhaps, we are rude and difficult with ourselves. And when someone takes us for granted, it's an opportunity to explore where we may be undervaluing our own self-worth."

Realization dawned on me as I pondered the implications. "So, those times when I've felt down and criticized myself, I can attribute it to being 'rude to myself'?" I sought confirmation.

Nandini nodded, acknowledging the truth in my words. "Indeed. It's a matter of perspective. Building a better relationship with yourself should be the first step."

Lost in thought, I contemplated the significant effort that lay ahead. "It seems like there's yet another challenge I need to overcome," I confessed.

Nandini's warm smile reassured me as she offered words of encouragement. "Remember, progress often comes with some discomfort," she said. "Now, let's discuss the main cause of unhappiness: 'Stamping.'"

"Stamping?" I raised an eyebrow, curious about the term.

Nandu nodded thoughtfully, her gaze fixed on the swirling patterns in her tea. "Yes, stamping, also known as stereotyping, occurs when you pass judgment on an event or person without considering all the facts and relying solely on your own perception. It's like creating a story based on incomplete information."

Captivated by her explanation, I asked for an example.

She smiled knowingly. "Imagine you go to a restaurant where the waitress seems a little uncomfortable and annoyed. In your mind, you believe the waitress is displeased with your outfit and judging you. You create a narrative and stamp it with judgment, thinking, 'She must be judging my fashion.'"

Recalling a similar experience from my own life, I nodded in agreement. "Yes, sometimes I feel like people judge my style because it's unique."

Nandu's eyes sparkled with understanding. "Exactly. We often create these stories out of ignorance, beginning from childhood. Our environment, family, and upbringing shape these fictional narratives. And unknowingly, we start living our lives based on these false assumptions, which breed unhappiness within us. However, we don't always know the whole story. Perhaps the color of your outfit reminded the waitress of a bad memory, or something unpleasant had happened to her just before you arrived. Yet, we create stories in our minds and make assumptions about things we don't fully understand. In reality, you might be a little insecure about your own fashion choices, which leads you to assume others are judging you. Think back to what happened with your friends from your old job. After meeting them again, you discovered they were actually speaking positively about you to others, never turning their back on you."

"You're right. Whenever I heard them whispering to each other, I assumed they were saying negative things about me behind my back. It didn't occur to me until recently that they were trying to be considerate and avoid triggering bad memories. They were trying to help me in their own way by checking up on me. But because of my own insecurities about keeping a job, I interpreted their actions as taunting." Pausing for a moment, I looked Nandini in the eyes. "So, how do we break free from this cycle of…… stamping?"

Nandini's voice was filled with wisdom. "The first step is to identify the stamping. Calmly ask yourself what exactly is bothering you.

Summarize the behavior that upsets you in a statement. For example, a father troubled by his children's messiness might stamp it as 'My children are irresponsible and disorganized.' Then, in Step 2, you introspect. Once you've recognized the stamping, turn the focus back on yourself and explore different aspects of your own life. Ask yourself questions, such as whether you're irresponsible in other areas like fulfilling your family duties or whether you're organized in financial planning."

I nodded, beginning to see the pattern. "So, it's about reflecting on myself and discovering where I exhibit the same stamping in my own life."

"Exactly," Nandu affirmed. "You need to uncover those hidden areas where you project your stamping onto others. It can be quite revealing. Step 2 helps you recognize the similarities between your stamping and your own life, highlighting areas for improvement. In the example with the father, he may realize that the children were only mimicking his messy nature. But without introspection, he may have never come to that realization."

"So, what's the final step? What should the father do after this realization?" I asked eagerly.

Nandini took a deep breath. "Step 3 is to reassess and take action. You must see reality as it is, accepting it without biases. If your story is that someone is irresponsible and disorganized, reframe it to acknowledge that they simply don't keep a few things tidy. More importantly, it is a call for corrective action on your own shortcomings."

Contemplating her words, I sensed a profound shift within me. "So, it's about perceiving reality neutrally without making assumptions and then taking appropriate action to work on my own blemishes?"

Nandu nodded. "Precisely. You can choose to communicate with the person, expressing your desire for cleanliness and orderliness.

Or you might decide to wait or take no action at all if you consider it not to be a significant issue. But whatever you choose, it should stem from a clear understanding of reality, not just an emotional outburst caused by stamping."

I realized that this could be challenging for many people, especially those who are non-confrontational. "But what if direct communication isn't easy?"

Nandini's gaze softened as she spoke. "In this situation, you have the freedom to choose how you respond. You can use safeguard words, which allow you to express your thoughts indirectly and maintain harmony."

Curious, I asked, "What are safeguard words?"

Nandini spoke in a compassionate tone, "Safeguard words are a way to communicate our thoughts and desires without hurting others. They enable us to express ourselves while ensuring that our words are received positively. The underlying message is that we still love and respect the person, regardless of the topic we're discussing."

Intrigued, I nodded and inquired, "How do we use safeguard words?"

Nandu kindly smiled and explained, "When expressing your opinion, it's important to preface it as your perspective, acknowledging that it may be limited and subject to potential error. By saying something like, 'This is what I feel from my limited perspective due to the following reasons, but I may be wrong,' you show humility and create an environment where the other person won't feel offended."

I contemplated her words, realizing the power of communicating with love and understanding. "So, it's about expressing ourselves while respecting the perspective and opinions of others."

Nandu's eyes sparkled warmly. "Exactly. True love is experienced through giving, not demanding. The people in our lives are not here to love us; they are here to remind us that we are the source of love. Love knows no bounds, and when we experience it fully, we feel an overwhelming desire to give unconditionally. It feels liberating to expect nothing in return."

Her words resonated within me, challenging my preconceived notions about love. "I've always thought of love as a give and take, a transaction. But what you're saying... it's profound."

Nodding, Nandini wore a gentle smile. "Indeed, many of us have been conditioned to seek love externally, constantly yearning for appreciation, consideration, and approval. However, true love emanates from within, and when we recognize that, we discover the key to unlocking profound joy and contentment."

I sat in awe, realizing the depth of my own neediness and longing for validation. "You're right. I've spent so much of my life seeking external validation, always feeling incomplete, especially since I moved to this new city."

Nandini's voice softened. "Have you ever heard of Cognitive Dissonance?"

"Cognitive dissonance?" I asked, puzzled.

"Cognitive dissonance refers to the mental discomfort or tension that arises when an individual holds conflicting beliefs, attitudes, or values, or when their behavior contradicts their beliefs or values. It occurs when there is an inconsistency or discrepancy between thoughts, beliefs, or attitudes within a person's mind. For example, if someone believes that smoking is harmful to health but continues to smoke, they experience cognitive dissonance—a discomforting feeling. However, if they don't recognize this as the source of their discomfort, they might find other excuses for the unpleasant feeling. Cognitive dissonance also occurs when we feel insecure or uncertain."

"But why does uncertainty cause dissonance?"

Nandu explained, "We have a natural inclination to seek complete information because it makes us feel safer and more in control of our environment. Incomplete information or unresolved situations create uncertainty. This is why people instinctively fear the dark—we feel a lack of control or ignorance about our surroundings. Incomplete situations introduce uncertainty, presenting us with unknown variables, unpredictable outcomes, or a lack of clarity about the future. This uncertainty can be unsettling because it reduces our ability to anticipate and plan effectively. Our minds prefer certainty as it provides stability and allows us to feel more in control of our lives. In an attempt to regain a sense of control, our minds often seek closure or resolution. We may engage in behaviors such as gathering more information, making assumptions, or trying to find quick solutions."

"But doesn't that mean we'll always feel incomplete and jump to conclusions? Isn't it ingrained in us?"

Nandu responded, "Not necessarily. Understanding that our knowledge is limited fosters humility and open-mindedness. It reminds us that there is always more to learn and discover. With this mindset, we become more receptive to new information, alternative perspectives, and the possibility of evolving understanding. Instead of rigidly clinging to incomplete information or preconceived notions, we remain open to the idea that there may be gaps in our knowledge that need to be filled. We become more comfortable with uncertainty and incompleteness, recognizing that not every question has an immediate answer and not every situation can be neatly resolved. This increased tolerance allows us to hold multiple possibilities or perspectives in mind without immediately seeking closure. It enables us to navigate complex and incomplete situations with greater flexibility and adaptability."

Nandini continued speaking, her voice flowing naturally. "When you express your true thoughts and feelings, it brings closure and a sense of satisfaction and happiness," she said. "Even small acts of completion can prevent remorse and incompleteness from tainting your departure from this world."

Her words struck a chord within me, and I couldn't help but express my concern. "I don't want to leave this world with regrets."

Nandini's comforting voice reassured me. "None of us do. That's why it's important to start with small steps. Tie up loose ends and unfinished matters in your life, one by one. This will lead you towards completeness in every aspect of your existence."

I sat there, deep in thought, realizing the truth in her words. It made sense. In situations where we feel incomplete or lack the full picture, we often make assumptions or seek more information. I noticed this happening frequently while driving, where I would assume that a speeding driver was reckless without considering that they might be dealing with an emergency. If I had considered their perspective, I could have accepted the situation easily and avoided unnecessary frustration.

Nandini continued, her voice filled with introspection. "There could be many incomplete things in your life that you might not even realize. If you examine your daily activities, you'll find that many of them remain unfinished."

I reflected on the fragments of tasks that lingered unresolved in my daily life.

"This is why we experience dreams at night," Nandini continued. "Those unfinished tasks seek completion through our dreams. Pay attention to whether these incomplete matters bring peaceful sleep or disturb your rest. Do you wake up feeling refreshed or mentally exhausted?"

I let out a sigh, realizing the truth behind my restless nights. "For the past few months, I haven't been sleeping peacefully. Now I understand that it's the incompleteness in my life that haunts me. I should start by listing all the incomplete activities and work towards completing them. Maybe that will bring me a sense of wholeness."

Nandini nodded approvingly, her eyes filled with encouragement. "Indeed, completing those unfinished tasks will undoubtedly contribute to your sense of wholeness. However, it's equally important to bring completion to your relationships. Open and honest communication is essential to achieving fulfillment in your connections with others."

Curiosity sparked within me, and I leaned closer, eager to learn more. "How can I ensure completion in my relationships through communication?"

Nandini smiled, her gentle demeanor putting me at ease. "Before seeking completion, create an atmosphere where the other person can listen without bias or prejudice. You might start by saying, 'I'm not sure how best to express what's on my mind. Should I speak or keep it to myself?'"

She continued guiding me through the process. "'I only want to share how I am feeling about the situation; it doesn't mean someone is wrong or right.' By framing the conversation this way, you give the other person an opportunity to be supportive and respond with, 'It's okay, speak your mind as you wish.'"

I absorbed her words, realizing the power of vulnerability and openness in building stronger connections. "To resolve any conflicts with a family member or friend, I need to open my heart and initiate the conversation. I can start by saying, 'There's something that has been weighing on my mind for several days, and I haven't been able to mention it. But today, I want to talk to you about it.'"

Nandini paused, her eyes reflecting deep understanding. "Begin with words like, 'I am really sorry. I don't mean to criticize you because I could be quite wrong, but I want to offer my perspective to achieve closure.' Once you've set this foundation, you can express what has been suppressed in your mind."

I listened intently, realizing the importance of such communication in building stronger connections. "By seeking closure in this way, I can let go of burdens, avoid dishonesty or unnecessary lies, and fulfill everyone's needs and desires. It's about bringing things to completion. And when we master the art of closure, our minds can let go of the past and the future, finding fulfillment in the present."

My mind raced with questions, eager to understand every aspect. "Nandini, what if things don't go as planned? I often struggle to find the right words and end up making matters worse."

Her comforting voice assured me, "When physical communication becomes difficult, subjective communication can be a valuable tool."

Curiosity sparked within me, and I asked her, "What is subjective communication?"

Nandini's eyes gleamed with a sense of mystery. "It is a means of communication through the subconscious mind. Our subconscious minds are intricately connected, like the branches of a tree. You can mentally communicate your feelings and words to another person by inviting them into your field of attention. You don't need to speak physically; instead, address them in your mind as though they can listen. It may sound peculiar, but it truly works. Our subconscious mind is pure and innocent compared to our conscious mind. That's why subjective communication is more effective when the conscious mind is tired and unproductive, like when the other person is sleepy or fatigued. Whatever we suggest in that state is easily received and accepted by the other person. To help you grasp the concept, consider that hypnotism is based on subjective communication."

A sense of wonder filled me as I contemplated this unconventional form of connection. "Wow! It sounds both intriguing and challenging. Though it might be difficult to grasp fully, I'm tempted to give it a try," I admitted, my skepticism mingling with genuine curiosity. My eagerness to explore new possibilities was palpable.

"If you're skeptical, let's think about it differently. Do you know what influences people the most during a conversation or a speech?"

"Is it how well they speak?"

"That's just a part of it. According to Mehrabian's communication model, only 7% of the meaning is conveyed through words, 38% comes from vocal tone, and 55% from nonverbal cues like facial expressions, gestures, and body language."

A lightbulb went off in my mind. "Do you mean those moments when best friends or couples seem to know what the other is thinking or planning without even saying a word?"

Nandini's smile brightened. "Exactly! With subjective communication, you can start by seeking forgiveness within yourself and then extend it mentally to the other person. This sets the healing process in motion, including the restoration of relationships. Once you've sought forgiveness, you can freely express your thoughts and emotions."

Nandini nodded, her eyes filled with assurance. "Patience and persistence are key. If you still feel uneasy, keep practicing subjective communication. Eventually, you'll experience a shift."

A flicker of hope ignited within me as Nandini shared her personal experiences. "You'll begin to feel a sense of completeness within yourself. When you engage in conversation, you may find the other person more receptive, and the exchange will flow more smoothly. Practicing this method has worked wonders in most of my relationships, and I'm confident it will do the same for you."

Encouraged by her words, I made a commitment to give it a try. "I'll definitely practice it. In fact, I need to have a conversation with my colleagues. They have all been kind, but I'd like to get to know them better. I feel shy and don't know what to say, especially since they've known each other for so long."

Nandini nodded understandingly. "To many, this concept may seem overly simplistic and illogical to be true. However, thousands of people have practiced it and are reaping its benefits."

She continued, shifting the focus to another aspect of completion. "There's another facet of 'completion' I'd like to share. It's not just about discussing negative matters; positive aspects can also be conveyed. If you like someone's qualities, openly appreciate them. Many people experience others' positive traits throughout their lives but never openly admire them."

"For instance," Nandini elaborated, "if you have admired Reema's work ethic but never shared this with her, that uncommunicated feeling of appreciation can contribute to a sense of incompleteness. Therefore, if you admire her qualities, let her know. And if there's something you don't like, express it as well, but choose your words wisely. This is how you can achieve completeness in your relationship. Common sense should prevail in this process; completion is not meant to hurt anyone. With regular practice, relationships become stronger."

Expressing my gratitude to Nandini, I was overwhelmed by the realization that there were numerous people I had silently admired in my heart but never expressed it. "Nandini, I truly admire you and how you balance everything—home, career, and your child. Your dedication and sincerity are inspiring, and witnessing your commitment to each task fills me with joy. You have achieved a harmonious balance in all aspects of your life, and you radiate happiness and contentment. I can't find the exact words to thank you for everything you've done for me in the past year. You pulled me out of the abyss I was caught in, helped me secure this job, and guided me toward a positive path. You have truly changed my life, Nandini," I concluded, my voice choked with emotion as tears welled up in my eyes.

Nandini playfully squeezed my hand, attempting to lighten the atmosphere. "Hey, come on, don't make me emotional," she teased. "The real thanks is due to my spiritual teacher, whom I met at the retreat. I regularly attend the weekly follow-ups and meditations, which equip me with invaluable knowledge."

Sniffing back my tears, I managed a weak smile. "Yeah. Someday, I would like to participate in this retreat that you keep mentioning."

"Now, let's take a break and order some ice cream. What do you say?" Nandini suggested with a contented sigh, diverting our attention to a moment of indulgence as we finished our lunch.

I nodded eagerly, grateful for the chance to savor a sweet treat with my dear friend. As we left the restaurant, I embraced Nandini tightly, feeling the joy of completion enveloping us both.

22

Planting the Seeds of Abundance

While browsing gifts for Reema's birthday, I felt a pang as I looked at my bank account. Sometimes, I'm just not sure what to do. I've spent so carelessly in the past that now I'm struggling to maintain that lifestyle. I shared my thoughts with Nandini during our weekly cooking sessions.

"Nandu, I have spent so much money recklessly on parties and buying all sorts of needless things that I hardly use," I confessed, my voice heavy with regret. "I feel awful that I have not been handling my finances well. My job at Impression has helped me with my debts, but I don't have any extra money or savings."

"Financial well-being is an integral aspect of a balanced life," Nandini said thoughtfully. "It is an important aspect of living in the material world. I know this money problem formula, which was particularly helpful for me. Would you be interested in knowing about it? I am sure it can be helpful to you too."

I exclaimed with a glimmer of curiosity in my eyes. "Of course, I am all ears. But what's a money problem formula?"

A mischievous smile danced on her lips as she began to explain. "If money doesn't stay for long, then it is only because of our bad habits.

If we break these habits, the same money becomes a blessing."

Nandini's voice was filled with conviction. "Careless spending of money is one habit that is like poking a tiny hole in the bottom of a ship. This tiny hole can sink the whole ship. Some petty expenses could have formed holes in your 'life' boat."

She enthusiastically continued, "The money problem formula states: Carelessness + Laziness + Wrong Habits − Understanding = Money Problem. In simple terms, financial problems end for those who get rid of their addictions, carelessness, and laziness and raise their understanding of money. Else this trouble continues to plague people throughout their lives."

Curiosity piqued, I interjected, "By carelessness, do you mean squandering money?"

"Yes," Nandini affirmed. "The habit of carelessness and extravagant spending aggravates money problems. Financial troubles will continue as long as one lacks understanding about money. We should use money; money should not use us. Wealth has been created to support us so we can reach our highest potential; mankind has not been created to glorify wealth.

"Money is a means, not the end; it is a path, not the destination. No matter what we see around us, we should always believe that everything is abundant on earth, including money. This helps us stay positive, and this positive self-talk shifts our focus to abundance. And as I said before, what we focus on, and what our self-talk is, will be what the reality becomes. Hence, we should learn to respect money and not harbor feelings like jealousy or hatred towards it.

"Start maintaining a monthly record of cash inflow and outflow. Money cannot be channeled properly unless you have an account of each and every penny. Ask yourself exactly what happened to the money you got. Where and how was that money spent?"

"I've tried it before, but it just confused me," I complained, picturing stacks of papers and numbers that seemed overwhelming.

"Come on!" Nandini encouraged me. "Use the mantra of acceptance! Note your expenses daily in a diary. You can even enter your data in a spreadsheet or an app that does the number-crunching for you."

I pondered her words for a moment, realizing the importance of her suggestion. "Hmm…"

"This small step will give you clarity about your finances. Whatever has gone has gone. But now you can decide where and how your money should be spent henceforth."

"Yes! That's what I want, too," I resolved, determination shining in my eyes.

"To avoid further wealth woes in your life, make a budget. I create ten parts of my money and set aside one part as savings. I don't consider that part as mine. Usually, people don't save any money at all, while others first save money and then squander it at parties and unnecessary shopping. This unnecessary extravagance drains their cash reserves.

"Some people start saving, but on the very next happy occasion, they organize parties, buy things, and so forth. Thus, they spend away all their savings. They squander the interest earned on long-term savings and find themselves back in the same situation of paucity."

"This is exactly what has happened to me," I confessed, a tinge of regret coloring my voice. "I used to spend all my money on shopping and parties and then used to keep wondering where all my money had gone."

Nandini continued, her voice gentle but firm, "A person always complains about a shortage of time, despite having much time, because they do not know exactly how and where their time is spent.

Similarly, money flows in everyone's life, but most people remain ignorant about how and where they spend it.

"The tasks that consume most of our time are known as 'time killer' tasks. Likewise, the expenses that consume most of our money can be termed 'money killers.' Beware of such money killers. When I made a list of such money killers, I was shocked. But that helped me realize where my money was draining away. As you said, 'I don't know where my money went,' here is your solution."

A renewed sense of determination emerged as I leaned closer, eager to learn more. "I think I can identify those money killers. But can you tell me more about budgeting?"

"Sure," Nandini responded, her voice filled with encouragement. "Preparing a budget spreadsheet has its own benefits. It reveals our own extravagance, carelessness, and foolishness. After making a budget, I noticed that even after taking care of all my necessary expenses, I could save some money. Additionally, I was able to donate to charity."

"Charity?" I echoed, intrigued by her mention of giving back.

"Absolutely!" Nandini exclaimed, feeling a renewed sense of purpose. "This approach allows us to plant the seeds of positivity and abundance in our lives, nurturing a sense of fulfillment and well-being. Moreover, it presents an opportunity to make a meaningful impact in the lives of those less fortunate. Even a small contribution from our income can become a beacon of hope for someone trapped in despair and poverty. In essence, my budget becomes my ally, safeguarding my loftier aspirations from being overshadowed by trivial desires. By prioritizing and directing my resources wisely, I can pursue my deepest passions and fulfill the true purpose of my life. I refuse to reach the end of my journey with regrets, lamenting, 'I always held a higher ambition to... but I never spared the time or resources for it.'"

"So, if I feel my biggest wish remains unfulfilled, I should definitely start budgeting," I concluded, eager to take control of my finances.

Nandini nodded approvingly. "By documenting your budget, you can identify which desires can be fulfilled within the nine parts of your income. If you don't prepare a budget for yourself, then as soon as you get money, you start shopping."

A hint of concern crossed my face. "Does this mean I shouldn't do any shopping?"

Nandini shook her head. "No, that's not what I meant. Shop for things that you've budgeted for first. There is one more way to ensure this. The 'Need and Want technique.' This technique is very effective and has helped me a lot."

"Need and want?" I repeated, curious to learn more.

Nandini explained, "Anytime you go shopping, ask yourself, 'Is this my need or want?' Need denotes something you really require, without which you cannot survive or progress. Want means something the mind is fond of or the urge to buy something because someone else has bought it. You buy stuff that someone else has bought, which is unnecessary for you at that point in time."

Realization dawned on me. "Ah! I remember I've done that often. I bought expensive dresses just because my friends would buy them and because I wanted to prove that I was no less. But I would hardly ever wear them," I admitted, feeling slightly embarrassed.

Nandini smiled sympathetically. "That's pretty common. Henceforth, while shopping, ask yourself, 'N or W? Is this a Need or a Want?' If the response is 'W,' then ask the next question, 'Have I already fulfilled all my needs like the house rent, bills, groceries, medicines, or other important expenses?' Fulfill those needs first."

I raised an eyebrow, seeking clarification. "Does that mean that if it is a want, I should never purchase that thing?"

Nandini reassured me. "Of course not, Esha! It doesn't mean that wants should never be catered to. But first, you need to take care of your necessities and set aside a decided amount for your savings before considering your wants. You will be surprised to see that most of your money troubles can get resolved just by asking the question, 'N or W?' Because after asking this question, only needful and right purchases are made. This has been my personal experience. By asking this question, I could curtail so many extravagant expenses."

Nandini continued to share her wisdom. "We often make big sacrifices very easily but are not alert when smaller wants arise. Trying to fulfill all minor wants, we remain devoid of our supreme goal. So, in a nutshell, you have to decide which of your desires you want to fulfill. With your budget, you can fulfill your needs. All your needs can fit easily into the nine parts of your income."

Listening intently, I soaked in Nandini's words, realizing that money held a deeper significance than just a means of acquiring material possessions. "Money is a means, not the end goal," she emphasized, "use it to reach your ultimate goal of attaining true happiness, which is permanent. The happiness derived from material possessions is temporary. People do not know that the words they speak gradually generate similar kinds of feelings inside them. Positive feelings attract money towards them while being depressed and worried about money diverts money away from their lives."

I listened intently, captivated by Nandini's explanation. "Focus on good feelings and change the definition of money in your mind: 'There is an abundance of everything for everyone.' This is the law of abundance. Be it money, time, love, happiness, or prosperity—everything is abundant in nature. These words will have a positive impact on your feelings. Good feelings are like a magnet; they attract all the good things into your life."

Curiosity got the better of me, and I couldn't help but ask, "How can you say that money is abundant in nature?"

Nandini smiled, ready to enlighten me. "It's not easy at first to see abundance if you're used to seeing lack. But think about it, whenever there is a need—for energy, for example—mankind has always come up with a solution. Innovators tap into their intuition for answers to problems. Otherwise, environment friendly energy sources like solar energy, wind energy, hydroelectric power, or nuclear energy would not have been discovered and harnessed."

She continued, "The point is that there was a need for energy, and while those who believed in scarcity started hoarding and controlling wood, coal, and oil, those who did not have such a mindset of scarcity found alternatives and learned how to harness renewable resources such as wind and solar energy."

Nandini's enthusiasm was contagious. "The universe is teeming with unlimited possibilities! The world in which we live is wonderfully obliging. The supreme creative potential makes it possible to fulfill the wishes of everyone simultaneously. Allow 'faith in abundance' rather than 'fear of scarcity' to steer your life."

"Abundance," I repeated, savoring the word.

Nandini nodded. "Isn't it? Imagine everyone is connected to the Universe through a pipe. Through that pipe, everything that we need is flowing—health, wealth, love, joy, prosperity, and everything else we can conceive. Then, a negative thought enters the mind. It could be a doubt about well-being or a notion of scarcity. When we entertain a negative thought or self-doubt, we, in effect, are placing a pebble in that pipeline. This pebble disrupts the flow of abundance.

"While one negative thought may not completely clog the pipeline, it does manage to slow it down to some extent. If we continue to think more of such negative thoughts, we can imagine that soon the pebbles will be clogging more of the flow. With enough negative thinking, it won't take long before the pebbles turn into rocks, stopping that natural flow of bounty.

"If we don't harbor a single negative thought, that's enough. We will automatically be propelled toward physical vitality, mental growth, social harmony, and financial abundance. We must ensure that our focus is always on the positive rather than the negative."

A surge of excitement coursed through me as the realization of the power of abundance sunk in. "Wow! I never thought of this," I exclaimed. "It gives such a nice feeling as soon as we say everything is abundant. The example you gave made it clear."

Nandini smiled warmly. "Money is a symbol of things that come into your life. The purpose of money is to make transactions simple and convenient. But people have forgotten the purpose of money. Money has become the ultimate goal today."

I listened intently, eager to learn more about how to embrace abundance. "After understanding the profundity of this law of nature, that everything is in abundance, you will easily be able to give when someone asks you for something, be it charity, cooperation, assistance, time, love, attention, or even money."

The idea of being able to give freely resonated with me. "All these donations will give you a sense of fulfillment. You will easily be able to make donations of money, too, because you have set it aside in your budget, and it has also been documented. If you keep working diligently to plant seeds of abundance with full faith and regularity, irrigating it with savings, then very soon it will grow up to become a giant tree of prosperity."

I envisioned the magnificent tree of prosperity, its branches reaching out in all directions. "Under the shade of this tree, you can then meditate, enjoy, and rest, as well as become an inspiration for others to walk on the path of prosperity. Whatever you give definitely comes back to you in multitudes. So, with the law of abundance, whatever you give, even money, will also come back to you manifold."

Feeling empowered, I voiced my immediate aspirations. "For now, I would like to solve all my money troubles first, pay off my debts, experience the abundance, and then later think of charity."

Nandini agreed, understanding my current circumstances. "Yeah, that's good enough for now. We can lead a life of abundance with the power of faith. We need to eliminate our false beliefs about money. Let's thank the universe for this abundance by being in the feeling of gratitude. When you're grateful for everything, you automatically move away from doubts, worries, and feelings of scarcity."

I realized gratitude was the key to unlocking the abundance that surrounded us. "When you are constantly in the feeling of gratitude, you automatically focus on the best, and therefore, you will receive the best! Gratitude makes you receptive to the unfolding of your highest possibilities. Gratitude removes the feelings of fear and worries that come with the belief of scarcity and competition."

Inspired by Nandini's wisdom, I acknowledged our common desire for financial stability. "We all want to have ample money in our life, but in ignorance, we still feel a deficiency of money at all times."

Nandini emphasized the transformative power of understanding. "No one becomes rich by earning money. One becomes rich by attaining an understanding of money. The right understanding of money destroys the very root of money troubles. As soon as this root is uprooted, the lack of wealth disappears from your life."

Feeling a renewed sense of purpose, I committed to myself. "I will soon stabilize my finances, pay off my debts, and support Dad instead of being a burden on him." I promised Nandini, "Nandu, I will work on the aspects we discussed today. I have even noted them down. Also, with this new understanding, I will now be able to plan things in a better way. Today's advice will also help me to plan for Reema's birthday in a better way, and you are going to help me with that."

Nandini beamed, ready to assist me on this transformative journey. "Of course... I'm at your service, ma'am."

A surge of optimism flowed through me as I embarked on this path of financial stability and abundance. With Nandini's guidance and the power of faith, I knew I had the tools to shape my financial future and make a positive impact in the lives of others.

Nandini and I bid each other farewell, grateful for our conversation and shared insights. I expressed my gratitude profusely, knowing that her guidance would have a lasting impact on my life. With a renewed sense of purpose, I left her house and stood on the bustling city street, waiting for a cab to take me to the train station.

As I stood there, a realization struck me. Nandini's advice about money echoed in my mind, and I made a spontaneous decision. Instead of taking a cab, I chose to walk to the train station, embracing the opportunity for a leisurely stroll. I had even cultivated a habit of coming in early to the office and leaving early, which meant I could avoid the usual evening rush.

That night, after completing my usual routine, I sat down with my diary and took a deep breath. Determined to take control of my finances, I created a budget and meticulously listed my pending debts. Dividing my salary into ten equal parts, I decided to allocate one portion to savings. Clearing my debts became my priority, and I was determined to put in as much as possible.

The following day was the weekend, and Reema and I had a routine of doing the groceries together. As we sat for breakfast, I excitedly shared my newfound "Money Mission" plan with Reema. She suggested we explore a nearby wholesale market to procure our groceries at a lower cost. With a shared sense of purpose, we set out to find the best deals.

After completing our grocery shopping, we found ourselves near a bustling mall. As we entered, I couldn't resist the allure of the clothing section. My eyes were immediately drawn to a beautiful denim dress, and my hand instinctively reached out to grab it. But just as I was about to indulge, a voice inside me reminded me of Nandini's advice—N or W. I engaged in a mental debate, battling the temptation to make an impulsive purchase.

Despite the allure of the sale and the fleeting desire for the dress, I reminded myself of my financial goals. I knew that succumbing to such temptations would hinder my progress. With a sigh, I reluctantly returned the dress to its rack, consoling myself that I could always purchase it once I had overcome my financial challenges.

N or W continued to guide me as I perused the makeup, jewelry, and accessories sections. These were the areas where I had previously fallen into the trap of unnecessary spending. Surprisingly, my cart remained empty except for a simple kohl eyeliner. I couldn't help but smile as I approached the cashier. My bill would have amounted to thousands in the past, but today, it was a mere fraction, thanks to Nandini and her wisdom. Even Reema was astonished by my restrained purchases.

Arriving back home, I felt a sense of accomplishment and gratitude. I took a moment to send a heartfelt thank-you note to Nandini, expressing my appreciation for her invaluable guidance. The savings were already piling up, and I marveled at my progress.

23

The Recipe for Perfect Health

Life had finally taken a turn for the better. Nandini had proven to be a blessing in disguise. Every moment spent with her filled me with gratitude and tranquility.

After neglecting my health for what I felt like an eternity, I finally went for a medical checkup. The next day, the phone rang, and it was Nandini's voice on the other end, inviting for a special lunch at her home. As I headed towards her home, I collected my reports.

"Nandu, do you have any wisdom to share about health issues?" I inquired while browsing my reports.

"What health issues?" she responded, clearly unaware.

"I received my medical check-up results today. My sugar levels are teetering on the edge!"

"Really?" she exclaimed, concerned.

"Yes, I need to take action now, or else I might end up with diabetes."

"Oh my God, that takes me back to when I faced a similar issue. Have you first accepted the results?"

I couldn't help but smile, taking a deep breath and gesturing with my fingers around my wrist, "Yep, that is the first thing I did when I saw the results. It really has been helping me keep calm in situations when I would have otherwise lost my cool." I sighed and continued, "For the past two years, my weight has steadily increased. I feel devoid of energy. Even my skin and hair have lost their luster. I've neglected my health for far too long. Is there anything I can do to regain it all? Do you have any tricks up your sleeve?" I asked, hoping for a solution.

"No more sweets for you from now on." Nandini giggled as she closed the lid on the box with biscuits, "Reduce your daily sugar intake and avoid refined sugar altogether. Follow a balanced diet, cut out sweets and fried foods, and you'll shed some weight," Nandini advised.

"I already know that… but it's just hard, you know?" I questioned skeptically.

"Yes, it's definitely hard. It's tried and tested by me. It's only temporary, Eshu. Once you have your sugar levels under control, you can indulge in moderation again. What did the doctor say?" she inquired.

"He gave me a list of dos and don'ts, like eating healthy—focusing on whole foods, aiming for at least 30 minutes of exercise every day, to try to lose weight. I must avoid sugary beverages, white bread, pasta, rice, sweets, and pastries. All the good stuff is off-limits," I lamented.

"To start off, focusing on eating wholesome foods, maintaining a healthy weight, and committing to some physical activity—whether it's a daily walk or two—can help bring your blood glucose levels back to normal," she suggested.

"Well, I had a similar problem. During college, my cholesterol levels had skyrocketed, serving as a wake-up call. That's when I decided to make lifestyle changes. I reduced my frequency of eating out and ordering in, switched to organic whole foods, and cut down on sugar and fat. I incorporated salads and fruits into my diet and made a habit of a regular forty-minute walk. It wasn't easy at first, as change never is. But challenges…" She trailed off.

"…are a doorway to growth," I finished the sentence, sharing a knowing smile.

"Yes! So, I regained my health in the process, gradually shed weight, and felt more fit. Now, I have increased stamina and energy. It really did help to have my husband by my side, adhering to the same rules; it gave me the additional support I needed. Additionally, you can start preparing your own meals, which should help you out financially. Just start implementing small things first, like a healthy breakfast in the morning."

"But mornings are always so rushed, Nandu," I complained.

"I understand that, but breakfast can be as simple as whole-grain cereal, almonds, and fruits or a healthy shake. It doesn't require much time," she reassured me.

"Fruits for breakfast? That doesn't sound appetizing!" I grumbled.

"Well, you already know how to break habits, right? Remember the 3Ds? You succeeded in conquering your alcohol habit, so this should be a piece of cake compared to that," she replied.

"Hmm…" I pondered. Why did I always have to struggle with bad habits in the first place and then work so hard to replace them with good ones? It felt like an ongoing battle.

"Also, choose a time that suits you and engage in any form of exercise you enjoy, doing it consistently. Even if it's just ten minutes, to begin with, persistence is the key to success," Nandini advised.

"Yeah, I've tried exercising in the past. I make resolutions every night, but something always comes up in the morning—a sudden project or difficulty getting out of bed. How do I deal with that?" I expressed my frustration.

"Now, that's the million-dollar question. That's something you can only overcome with daily practice. Do you maintain a regular sleep schedule?" Nandini inquired.

"No, it varies all the time," I confessed.

"Can you minimize the variation? Is there a specific time you usually sleep?" she probed.

"It usually gets late because I end up chatting on the phone or browsing the internet. Nowadays, I stay up late browsing Facebook or Instagram," I admitted.

"Hmm... those are all things that need to be controlled," Nandini raised an eyebrow.

"I know! But it's easier said than done. By the time I reach home, it's already late, and that's the only time I get to relax. Are you going to take that away from me too?" I grumbled.

"It's not me, it's you. Unless you want diabetes," Nandini remarked with a hint of sternness.

"Uhhh... don't remind me," I sighed in exasperation.

"If you prioritize sleeping on time, you won't have to worry about when to wake up. Now, there are a few tips to help you wake up. Would you like to hear them?" Nandini offered.

"Of course, I'm all ears," I responded.

She smiled appreciatively. "That's great! Well, you can try drinking a lot of water before going to bed. That might help wake you up."

"I have tried that once," I admitted. "But after using the restroom, I went back to sleep again."

She pondered for a moment, then said, "Hmm...okay. After the alarm, you can do the following things: Immediately throw away your blanket, switch on the light, remember your ultimate goal, play your favorite music, pray, splash water on your face, drink water, and tell yourself, 'I can seize the day!'"

I chuckled at the long list of "to-do's" she proposed. "That seems like a lot," I remarked. "Have you tried it?"

"Yes, it works!" she replied eagerly. "I immediately splash water on my face. There's also a final motivation that should get you out of bed quickly."

Curiosity piqued, I asked, "What's that?"

"Well, if you don't get up on the scheduled time, that day you go on a 'fast,'" she said mischievously.

"Nandini! Does your torture ever end?" I exclaimed, half-jokingly.

"Easy! That's the final step," she said, grinning. "In case everything else fails, what do you say? Are you ready for the challenge?"

"Do I even have an option?" I responded. My health was at stake here, and I had finally realized its importance.

"Well, willpower plays an important role too!" Nandini emphasized. "Without the will to be healthy, one cannot become healthy. Those who are facing health issues will no doubt work for better health; they don't have any option. But even if we are already healthy, we should kindle our will to raise our health quotient consistently, preparing the mind and body for higher expressions of life."

"Persistence, yeah?" I nodded.

"Yes, it's a continuous process," she confirmed. "And don't be under the illusion that your health will never improve. Many times, people are told that the disease they suffer from is chronic and incurable. They believe that they have an incurable disease and try various therapies, only to find that the disease still persists."

Nandini's voice lowered, and she leaned in closer. "There is indeed a remedy for such diseases deemed incurable. When a disease is said to be incurable, it only means that now the cure for the disease exists within you! External remedies will not help you anymore. You need to draw out the remedy from within and put it into effect persistently."

"Remedy inside us? How is that possible?" I asked, genuinely intrigued.

"It's called the placebo effect. There are many cases where the belief in the treatment's effectiveness influences our subjective experience of pain. In research studies, a particular group of participants does not receive the treatment, but they do not know this. They think they also received the treatment and sometimes start getting better. This is because they believe they are getting better and actually start to get better."

"People hold onto the assumption, 'I am a sickly body with the disease.' When we hold onto the belief of disease and give it attention, we keep the disease alive."

"Really?" I questioned, finding it difficult to accept such a notion.

"Think about it; it is said that the human body replaces billions of cells every day. If our body is constantly changing and renewed, why does one continue to be sick? Nature is doing its best by changing and renewing the body, but man preserves the disease," Nandini explained. "When we constantly repeat certain thoughts, they get reinforced within our subconscious mind as beliefs. Beliefs are like roofs. A roof cannot stand by itself; it needs pillars."

I listened intently, trying to grasp the concept.

"All this is new to me and a bit difficult to digest," I admitted.

"I understand that," she reassured me. "You see, the roof of belief needs pillars of evidence. Without the pillars of evidence, the roof of beliefs will collapse. The more evidence you acquire, the more pillars you provide for the roof of the belief, and the stronger the belief becomes. This is why when facing a serious disease, doctors always tell you to keep a positive attitude. Eventually, the belief becomes so strong that we sincerely convince ourselves that it becomes our undisputable truth."

I nodded, slowly comprehending her analogy. "So, in the case of diseases, we need to convince ourselves that the body in which the disease was present is no longer there. We can use positive self-talk every day, telling ourselves, 'Now, I have a healthy body…The effect of the disease is no longer there…I am now free from this disease.'"

"But for that to work, you really have to believe in this thing, right?" I questioned.

"Yes, you need to have conviction for the self-talk to work," she affirmed, a gentle smile on her lips.

"There is also another angle to this," Nandini continued. "At times, we experience that an illness persists for a long period, and no known remedy seems to work. We might have tried all possible remedies and therapies to no avail. Also, there may be no visible reason for the occurrence of the illness or disorder. In most probability, the disease could be caused by our own hidden need to remain ill."

I furrowed my brow, unable to comprehend why anyone would want to remain ill.

"We never want illness consciously," she clarified. "But a hidden need may exist within us, unknown to us, which continues to cling onto the illness. When we release the hidden need, the illness begins to dissolve miraculously."

She paused, allowing her words to sink in. "As the child grows up, there could still be some childhood notions, some hidden needs that they may have felt as a child, due to which they experience a sense of safety by clinging onto a particular illness. This illusory sense of security manifests as a hidden need to cling to problems, to hold onto illnesses. Some even claim to have a mental illness since it brings them comfort to feel like there is a reason for their negative feeling despite not having the symptoms."

Nandini sensed my astonishment and proceeded to provide an example. "Jaya, my colleague, was fed up with her obesity. She weighed 85 kg and had tried her best to lose weight. She had joined a weight-loss program at the gym, consulted a dietician, followed a strict diet, and improved her workout routine. Despite all her efforts, she was unable to lose much weight. The weighing scale still showed 84 kg.

'When she was told that she may have a hidden need to remain obese, she initially rejected this idea. But as she agreed to look within and reflect deeply, she discovered that she had a belief that obesity helped her in appearing less attractive. It was a learned way that her subconscious mind had adopted to avoid marriage, which her parents were insisting on."

Nandini continued, painting a vivid picture. "Since childhood, Jaya had observed the difficult circumstances her mother had to endure to continue the marriage and bring up the children. Obesity became a hidden need for Jaya to avoid married life. It was also her way of feeling secure without being noticed as an eligible bachelor."

The revelations stunned me, and I contemplated my own hidden needs and desires. There was a lot to process, "So, sort of how I took to alcohol to feel socially accepted. I did not want to stop drinking even though I knew how bad it was because I was scared that people would not find anything interesting in me. I kept drinking despite how bad it made me feel, just so I could avoid being true to myself; I was intentionally making myself ill despite knowing the truth.

"Oh God, all this is so weird," I exclaimed, my mind racing with newfound understanding. "What if I, too, have any hidden need?

But my problem is that I have not even tried consistently to lose weight. But I am surely going to try sincerely from here on out."

"The average human body is made of 70 percent water," she said. "Since we are primarily made of water, and water can be influenced by positive and negative energy, it becomes all the more vital that we re-look at our thoughts and feelings."

Nandini went on to share her practice of praying before drinking water or consuming food to ensure positive vibrations were present in what we consumed. She believed that by doing so, we could fill ourselves with positivity, satiety, and peace. I recalled the times I had seen her silently offer a prayer before every meal, and now I understood the reason behind it. It was a small step, but one that held profound meaning. "I, too, will start implementing this habit from now onwards and will pray before eating or consuming water," I declared.

Nandini smiled, acknowledging my decision. "Yes, it may seem simple, but it can take you a long way toward positivity and good health," she reassured me. Her words intrigued me, and I wanted to learn more about these practices that could shape our well-being.

"You can also try positive affirmations for health purposes," Nandini continued, reminding me of our previous discussions. "It's like positive self-talk." I nodded, recalling our conversations on the power of affirmations.

Nandini explained that when we repeated these affirmations consistently, our body and mind became programmed to experience complete health. She emphasized that when the body and mind accepted and firmly believed in something, it would manifest in our lives. Repetition of new healthy beliefs was the secret to reprogramming the mind, replacing the old belief patterns.

"To put positive words to use, consciously and lovingly repeat them," Nandini advised. "Memorize these positive belief statements by heart so they can be instilled into the subconscious mind." She suggested practicing these affirmations in a relaxed posture, either sitting on a chair or lying on the bed, as the potency of spoken words increased when the body was relaxed. Nandini even suggested turning these affirmations into a poem, making them more memorable and enjoyable.

She further recommended another method of reinforcing these beliefs. "Pick one or two affirmations and write them in your diary 10 to 20 times. Read them aloud and give them a little tune and rhythm so that you can joyfully hum them," Nandini explained. "By continuously focusing on these new beliefs, they will manifest in your reality."

Nandini jotted down a list of health-infusing affirmations that she used, encouraging me to choose the ones that resonated the most with me. As I read through the list, I felt a surge of inspiration and hope. These affirmations spoke of perfect health, increasing vitality, and taking care of my body. They painted a picture of a healthier and happier me.

But Nandini didn't stop there. She warned me about the dangers of negative self-talk, especially during challenging times. "When we indulge in negative self-talk and focus on negativity, it can attract a host of problems in life," she cautioned. She shared examples of self-defeating thoughts people often harbored, thoughts that strengthened fear within the body and manifested as imbalances in blood circulation. The consequences were lethargy and drained energy.

I inquired, "What exactly do you mean by negative self-talk? Are you talking about self-judgment?"

"That does fall into the category, but let's go back to the topic of weight, for instance," Nandini replied. "Imagine you have diligently committed to a routine for weeks but don't observe any visible changes. At that point, you may think, 'No matter what I do, I can't seem to lose weight. Maybe it's all just a waste of time.' This negative energy hampers your progress and invalidates the hard work you've put in. It becomes a counterproductive cycle. Remember, you must train not only your body but also your mind," she emphasized, pointing to her head.

Listening to Nandini's words, I realized how often I had fallen prey to such negative thinking. It was time to break free from this cycle and embrace a more positive mindset. I felt determined to change my thoughts, replace pessimism with optimism, and nurture my well-being from within.

Nandini's guidance opened my eyes to a new way of approaching life and health. I understood that water and I were interconnected, and by focusing on positive thoughts and beliefs, I could shape my reality. With renewed enthusiasm, I embraced the practices she shared and embarked on a journey toward holistic well-being, knowing that every step I took would lead me closer to a healthier and happier existence.

The weight of our conversation lingered in the air, tugging at my thoughts. Nandini had offered me some advice on how to break free from the self-defeating habits that had plagued me for far too long.

"I am familiar with some of these negative thoughts," I admitted, "and have been guilty of indulging in some of them from time to time. They do defeat us."

Nandini nodded knowingly, her eyes filled with empathy. "The way out is to simply focus on your health," she said. "Root out all negative or pessimistic thoughts. Remain alert. When negative thoughts arise, immediately shift your focus to affirmations of healthy and wholesome living."

Her words struck a chord within me. It was as if a light had been switched on, illuminating a path toward a brighter future. "Just start small," she mused. "Something simple like replacing soft drinks with tea and eventually transitioning to water," she chuckled. "So, you begin from tomorrow morning, in fact, from tonight by going to bed on time. Would you like me to call you initially as I prepare for my morning walk so you won't fall asleep again?"

I couldn't help but feel grateful for her unwavering support. "Sure, why not?" I replied. "I can do it with all the help I can get. Thanks!"

With our plans set, we finished our lunch. I took leave of Nandini and went to the office to catch up with some pending work. As evening descended, I left the office. It was a conscious effort to prioritize my well-being and make positive changes in my routine.

24

Step by Step

Arriving home on time, I was pleasantly surprised to find a burst of productivity within me. I managed to cook a simple yet nourishing meal for myself and Reema. When Reema returned from work, she was genuinely delighted to find dinner ready.

"Wow, Esha!" she exclaimed. "This meal is really good. But how did you come early today?"

A sense of pride swelled within me as I revealed my newfound determination. "Right," I replied, "I am making some changes to my lifestyle from now onwards. I'm going to implement 'early to bed, early to rise,' and I'm going to start by going for morning walks starting tomorrow."

Reema's eyes widened in surprise. "Really, Esha?" she asked. "But you are such a night person. Will you be able to do it?"

A smile played on my lips as I confidently declared, "Yes! I'm not a night person anymore, but rather a 'changed person' from now on."

"Good luck!" Reema responded, laughing.

As the night settled in, I thanked Reema for her company and retreated to my room. I needed to make a couple of calls before calling it a night. With my tasks completed, I slipped into bed earlier than usual. Repeating my resolution, I visualized myself taking a refreshing walk and settled into bed.

However, the change in routine took its toll. I found myself tossing and turning, my mind restless from the unfamiliarity of sleeping so early. It was a battle between my two sides—one longing to pull on the blanket and enjoy a few more minutes of sleep and the other reminding me of my commitment to change.

After what felt like an eternity, my alarm finally went off, disrupting the darkness of the early morning. My hand instinctively reached out to silence it, and for a moment, I contemplated pulling the blanket over my head. But then, I remembered Nandini's encouraging voice echoing in my mind.

"Push off your blanket!" it urged. "Please, just five minutes!" countered the opposing voice.

"No, get up now, please," the encouraging voice persisted. The battle within me intensified as doubts and excuses clouded my thoughts.

"I didn't get to sleep till my usual time;" I reasoned, "it's still dark."

"It's going to be light soon. If you don't succeed today, it will be the same story all over again. You have made a resolve," the encouraging voice reminded me. "Yes, you owe it to yourself," it whispered.

"Fine." With a surge of determination, I threw away my blanket and reluctantly climbed out of bed. Groggily, I made my way to the bathroom and splashed cold water on my face. The refreshing sensation awakened me, washing away the remnants of sleep.

Just as I was about to finish my morning routine, my phone rang. It was Nandini, cheerfully greeting me, "Good morning, sleepy head!"

I couldn't help but chuckle at her playful teasing. "Pretty soon, I am going to be slim again," I replied, feeling a newfound sense of optimism.

"I like that response," Nandini said warmly. "Good to see you up and about. Head out soon! We're heading out now. Good day!"

Feeling buoyed by her words, I ended the call and prepared to leave. Taking a thirty-minute walk in a nearby park, I relished the cool, crisp air that filled my lungs. But I found a new issue. Every few minutes, I felt the urge to just stop and go home and sleep.

Returning home, I found myself wanting to take another shower and go back to bed. I took my mind off of it by preparing a healthy breakfast for myself and even adding fruit to complete the meal.

A sense of accomplishment swept through me as I waved bye to Reema, "I am leaving now so that I can get back early and settle into my new routine. Good day!" I smiled, radiating the newfound joy that came from taking charge of my well-being.

"Bye!" Reema smiled back, her eyes filled with awe and admiration.

As I entered the office, my colleagues were shocked at my early arrival. Arriving ahead of schedule, I was determined to tackle the day's tasks. During my tea break, I shared my newfound plan of a daily pre-work walk with my coworker, Sanya. She confided in me about her own struggles: "I faced a similar challenge in college. I would force myself to go on jogs, but whenever I returned home, my loving mother would painstakingly prepare a lavish breakfast, and I would feel guilty about rejecting her efforts. Unfortunately, my lack of self-control often led to overeating, rendering my exercise efforts pointless."

Curiosity brimming within me, I asked, "So, how did you overcome that obstacle?"

Her response was simple yet ingenious. "I discovered a walking trail near my college," she revealed. "I could still wake up at the same time, but instead of going on a walk right away, I would go to college early and then go for a walk before attending my classes. This way, I created a physical and mental distance from the temptations without hurting my mom. Interestingly, I still follow a similar routine. A charming little park is just a five-minute stroll away from the office. You're more than welcome to join me in the mornings."

Her invitation touched me deeply, presenting a wonderful opportunity not only to forge a closer bond with my colleague but also to prioritize my well-being. Overjoyed, I exclaimed, "I'd absolutely love to!" Excitement filled the air as we solidified our plans to arrive at work an hour earlier, engaging in walks or jogs before starting the workday.

After work, I went to the grocery store and filled my basket with fresh fruits and vegetables, determined to nourish my body with wholesome food. Arriving home, I freshened up and tuned into my favorite songs, finding solace in their melodies as I prepared a healthy meal.

Reema arrived home later than usual, greeted by the aroma of the food I had prepared. Her gratitude warmed my heart, and I realized the joy of being able to do small acts of kindness for those I cared about. Seeing her happy made me happy, and as I set the alarm for the next day, I envisioned my resolve to continue on this path of transformation. With exhaustion from the day's early start and exercise, I quickly succumbed to sleep.

As the week went on, Sanya and I started our joint workouts. We would alternate between speed walking and jogging to ensure we weren't too tired for the workday, but surprisingly, the days I worked out more gave me more energy. The following day felt easier, as I had established a routine of sleeping on time. Despite the lingering aches and pains from my morning walk, I mustered the strength to complete my thirty-minute exercise. I seamlessly transitioned into my office routine and accomplished tasks before the rest of the staff arrived, relishing in the sense of achievement.

During lunchtime, tempting distractions in the form of sweets and fried snacks surrounded me, but I held fast to my diet plan. Each time I resisted the temptation, my resolve grew stronger.

One day, Sanya approached me with an unexpected invitation, her eyes shimmering with anticipation. "Hey Esha, care to join us for a drink after work?" she asked, unaware of my past struggles.

Her invitation triggered a flood of memories, reminding me of my former self, who would have readily accepted such an offer without hesitation. However, I had evolved, and alcohol no longer held power over me. Yet, a small part of me was concerned: What if my refusal jeopardized our morning walks? Would she be offended that I declined her kindness in inviting me to join her? After contemplating for a moment, I smiled, knowing what I must do. I gently declined her invitation, saying, "Thanks, but I don't drink anymore. Anyway, I have to go now. Goodbye!"

Leaving the office, a sense of pride washed over me, reinforcing my commitment to my personal growth. However, a small part of me still felt a trace of regret. Should I have explained my situation further to ensure Sanya wouldn't be upset? No, I reassured myself. I didn't owe everyone an explanation for my choices. If Sanya genuinely valued our friendship, she would respect and understand my decision. If not, well, I could always continue walking on my own. I shielded my heart from the nagging doubts that lingered, determined to stand firm in my convictions. I patted my own back, knowing I had made the highest choice in that situation.

25

Discovering the Middle Ground

As I eagerly waited for Reema to return home, I prepared a delicious meal in the kitchen. The aroma of spices filled the air, and I couldn't help but feel a sense of pride in the development of my culinary skills. I wanted everything to be perfect for our evening.

When Reema finally entered the front door, her eyes widened in surprise as she caught a whiff of the mouthwatering feast that awaited her. "Wow, Esha! This smells amazing! What's the occasion?" she asked, her voice filled with genuine admiration.

I beamed with delight, gesturing towards the table. "No occasion, really. It's been a long week, and I just wanted to treat us to something special," I replied, my excitement evident in my voice.

As we sat down to eat, the flavors danced on our tongues, and we relished every bite. The conversation flowed effortlessly, and we laughed and reminisced about old times. It was a perfect evening, and I couldn't have been happier.

Once we had finished our meal, the topic turned to my recent encounter with a coworker. I confided in Reema, telling her about the offer to go out for a drink and my conflicting emotions. "I felt good about rejecting the drink, but at the same time, I couldn't help but feel bad for turning down my co-worker," I explained, my voice tinged with uncertainty.

Reema listened attentively, her eyes filled with understanding. After a moment of thoughtful silence, she suggested, "Why don't we invite your co-worker over for dinner?" She said as she pointed to the kitchen. "That way, you can bond over something both of you would be comfortable with."

What a great idea! A dinner gathering would provide the perfect opportunity to build stronger connections with my new colleagues. "You know what, Reema? That's a great idea! Maybe I can even invite a few more co-workers and turn it into a dinner party," I exclaimed, my excitement growing.

A smile spread across Reema's face as she nodded in agreement. "Absolutely! It's a fantastic chance for you to showcase your incredible cooking skills and create a welcoming atmosphere for your new colleagues. Plus, it'll be a great bonding experience for all of you," she affirmed.

The idea of hosting a dinner party was both exciting and made me nervous. Being an extroverted person, I had been longing to form meaningful connections with my co-workers. The thought of having them over to my home filled me with anticipation. However, a twinge of anxiety gnawed at the back of my mind.

What if they rejected my invitation? I couldn't help but worry that declining their earlier offer to go out for a drink might have soured our relationships. I feared that my eagerness to connect might be met with indifference or, even worse, rejection.

Moreover, I had a dark past that haunted me—a time when partying had consumed my life, leading to addiction. I was now on a path of recovery, and I was scared that this event could trigger old habits, tempting me to return to my former self.

But despite these fears, I knew I had to take a chance. I wanted to overcome my anxieties and foster genuine connections with my co-workers. The prospect of hosting a dinner party held so much promise—a chance to showcase my growth and share a part of myself with those who mattered.

The following day, I sat at my desk, anticipation bubbling within me. It was time to extend the invitations to my co-workers, a chance to bridge the gap between us and forge genuine connections. With a sense of determination, I composed an email inviting them to join me for dinner at my apartment on Saturday. I carefully worded each line, hoping to convey my sincerity and eagerness to connect.

As I hit the send button, I was a mix of excitement and nervousness. Would they accept? Would they see my invitation as a genuine gesture or an act of desperation? I tried to push aside my doubts, reminding myself that I had taken the first step toward building the relationships I longed for.

To my immense relief, the responses trickled in, one by one, and each one carried the joyous news of their acceptance. They were excited to join me for dinner. Even my boss, Sanjay, whom I had thought might decline due to his reserved and stilted personality, replied with an enthusiastic confirmation. I couldn't believe my luck. It seemed that the universe was aligning in my favor.

With only a few days to prepare, Reema and I wasted no time in transforming our humble apartment into a warm and inviting space. During the weekend, we scoured the market, selecting beautiful decorations and vibrant flowers for a stunning centerpiece. Our shared background in fashion proved to be a valuable asset as we meticulously arranged every detail, creating an ambiance that would leave a lasting impression.

In the kitchen, we poured over cookbooks, carefully selecting dishes that would delight our guests' taste buds. We wanted to showcase my newfound culinary skills and create a hearty and healthy meal. Together, Reema and I chopped, stirred, and seasoned, our laughter filling the air as we bonded over the shared joy of preparing this special feast.

In the midst of our preparations, Nandini, called to deliver unfortunate news. She had come down with a severe cold and wouldn't be able to attend the dinner party. My heart sank as disappointment swept through me. Nandini's absence meant losing a familiar face in a sea of new connections, and it left me worried about whether I would be able to navigate the evening alone.

Recognizing my concern, Reema reassured me, her voice brimming with confidence. "Don't worry, Esha. I'll be right there by your side. You won't have to face anything alone. And remember, this is your moment to shine. Embrace it."

Her words offered me solace, reminding me that I had come a long way on my journey of self-improvement. I had already overcome countless obstacles, and this evening would be no different. With Reema's support and my newfound strength, I would be able to resist any peer pressure that might arise and stay true to myself.

As the evening of the dinner party drew nearer, excitement and nervousness intertwined within me. I had prepared a space where connections could be fostered, and friendships could bloom. It was my chance to showcase not only my cooking skills but also the person I had become—a person who sought genuine connections, who had emerged from the shadows of addiction, and who was ready to embrace life with open arms.

As the doorbell rang on that Saturday evening, signaling the arrival of my co-workers, I took a deep breath, feeling a surge of confidence and gratitude. It was time to welcome them into my home, share a meal, and create memories that would shape our relationships moving forward.

26

Echoes of a Restless Heart

I stood eagerly by the front door, my heart racing with a mix of excitement and nerves as I prepared to welcome our first guest. Tonight held special significance as it was an opportunity to connect with my co-workers on a deeper level. The faint sound of footsteps approaching the door made my anticipation grow. As we swung the door open, warm smiles and cheerful greetings greeted us, accompanied by the familiar sound of laughter. The living room quickly filled with animated conversations, and I felt a surge of joy as everyone settled comfortably on the cozy couches, discussing the upcoming bridal fashion show.

"Wow, Esha, you've done an amazing job with the decorations!" exclaimed Sanya, her eyes scanning the room in awe.

I blushed, grateful for the compliment. "Thank you! I wanted to create a welcoming atmosphere for all of you."

The evening flew by in a whirlwind of laughter, stories, and shared anticipation for the upcoming bridal show. We served a delightful dinner, and the tantalizing aroma of the food filled the air, tempting the taste buds. Each bite was savored not only for its flavor but also for the chance it provided to forge stronger bonds with one another. I was exhilarated that everyone enjoyed my cooking so much.

As the night progressed and our guests bid farewell, Reema and I found ourselves alone in our tidy yet silent house. With tired smiles, we exchanged glances, grateful for the successful evening we had just experienced. However, as I began tidying up, a subtle unease crept into my thoughts, tugging at the corners of my mind.

I closed the door behind our last departing guest, the echoes of my footsteps resonating through the quiet house. Reema joined me in the kitchen, and together we commenced the task of clearing away the remnants of our feast. Despite our chatter and the tidying, I couldn't shake off the nagging feeling that something was amiss.

As we completed the final dish, Reema yawned and stretched, her fatigue evident. "It was such a wonderful evening, Esha. I'm so glad everything went smoothly. We did an excellent job, didn't we?"

I nodded, a faint smile gracing my lips. "Yes, we did. Everyone seemed to have a fantastic time."

Reema studied my face, her brow furrowing with concern. "But you seem distant, Esha. Is something troubling you?"

I hesitated, struggling to articulate my emotions. "I don't know, Reema. It's strange. I anticipated feeling happy and fulfilled after tonight, but there's this lingering emptiness within me that I can't quite comprehend."

Reema's concern deepened, and she reached out to touch my arm. "Maybe it's simply exhaustion, Esha. We poured so much effort into this event. It's natural to feel drained afterward."

While her words held truth, I couldn't shake off the sensation that there was something more to it. I bid Reema goodnight and attempted to quiet my mind, but the uneasiness persisted.

The following day, I picked up the phone and dialed Nandini's number. My finger trembled slightly against the smooth buttons as I waited for her to answer, the anticipation and uncertainty intertwining within me.

The phone rang, each passing second heightening my nervousness. Finally, Nandini's familiar voice greeted me, infused with warmth and love.

"Eshu! How was last night?" Nandini exclaimed, her voice slightly hoarse.

"It was good... everything went smoothly," I replied, my tone lacking the expected enthusiasm.

Nandini, always attuned to my emotions, sensed that something was amiss. "Oh no, I know that tone. What happened?"

I hesitated, grappling with the conflicting emotions swirling within me. "Last night, we had this wonderful gathering at our place. The bridal show was the main topic, and everything went well. But Nandini, I didn't feel as happy as I expected. It's as if something is missing, and I can't quite comprehend why. I can't understand whether I'm becoming too sensitive or whether there's genuinely something wrong."

A heavy silence settled between us, punctuated only by our breaths. I could sense Nandini thoughtfully considering my words, searching for the right response.

Finally, her voice, gentle yet firm, broke the silence. "I understand. Have you tried using the acceptance mantra?"

"Yes, I repeated it several times last night. I'm not sure what I'm unable to accept because I'm not entirely sure what went wrong. I did accept that something doesn't feel right."

"That's a good start. You have work today, right? How about meeting up here for dinner later? We can delve deeper into your feelings and perhaps unravel this sense of unease together."

"Yes, please. I believe discussing it with you will help me better understand this lingering feeling."

"Great! See you tonight. And remember, continue using the acceptance mantra throughout the day. Perhaps it will reveal something within your heart."

"Thanks, Nandu; see you tonight," I said, ending the call.

I took a moment to gather myself before getting ready for work. Despite lacking the energy, I knew I had to go for a jog. Maybe it would distract me from these unsettling emotions. But goodness, I couldn't figure out why I felt so strange. Even the thought of seeing Sanya made me hesitate. What could be bothering me this much?

27

Beneath the Mask

I stepped into the office, my footsteps echoing in the quiet space, each sound amplifying the unsettling feeling that gnawed at my insides. It was a nagging uneasiness, an invisible weight. I couldn't shake off the persistent discomfort but could not put my finger on it. Why am I feeling so uncomfortable and hesitant to see my colleagues?

As I made my way toward my desk, I glanced at the clock, hoping that the passage of time would alleviate the unease. I had committed to exercising every morning with Sanya, a routine that had brought structure and energy to my life. But today, as I stared at the gym bag tucked away in the corner, I couldn't summon the usual motivation. The idea of going through the motions felt hollow and futile. However, a part of me recognized the importance of distracting myself from the whirlwind of thoughts swirling in my mind.

Summoning a smile that didn't reach my eyes, I approached Sanya. "Sanya, I'm feeling a little off today. Would you mind if we go on a short walk instead?" I asked, my voice tinged with the vulnerability I felt.

Sanya's face lit up with understanding and warmth. "Of course! I can imagine how drained you must be after putting so much effort into the party. A gentle stroll and some fresh air might be just what we need."

As we embarked on our walk, Sanya's words filled the air with enthusiasm. She spoke excitedly about her plans for the week, her gestures filled with genuine energy. While I listened, my attention was divided, my mind preoccupied with a sense of detachment. It was as if I were a passive observer, merely existing in the present moment while my thoughts wandered through the labyrinth of introspection.

Upon reaching a serene spot, we paused, and Sanya continued her animated chatter. However, her words were like distant echoes, their meaning lost in the whirlwind of my thoughts. I struggled to focus, a veil of detachment separating me from the world around me.

Feeling overwhelmed, I excused myself and walked off to a water fountain. I splashed cold water on my face, hoping the gentle touch would wash away the heaviness that weighed me down. Closing my eyes, I attempted to recite the acceptance mantra. But as I expressed the thoughts in my mind, I couldn't help but feel the hollowness of the recitation. It was a mere façade, an empty recital devoid of true acceptance. I realized that the mantra did not simply work by saying I must accept it. But what was it that I was not able to accept? Everything went fine at the party. What was it that I was struggling with? The more I thought about it, the more my head started to ache.

Returning to my desk, the weight of the unease still lingered, overshadowing the familiar surroundings. At that moment, Naina, a colleague I had connected with at the party, approached me. We had shared conversations about her love for horror movies and thrill-seeking adventures, and during our encounter, she had expressed a genuine desire to develop a friendship.

"Hey, Esha! Good morning!" Naina exclaimed, her voice filled with warmth and excitement. "Your party last night was incredible. We should spend more time together."

Forcing a smile, I greeted her, but the guilt intensified within me. I felt like a fraud, hiding behind a mask of social conformity, afraid to reveal my true self. "Yes, it was a fun evening. I'm glad you enjoyed yourself."

Naina leaned closer, her eyes sparkling with enthusiasm. "You know, while we were talking at the party, I couldn't help but think how much fun it would be to watch that new ghost movie together this weekend. What do you say?"

At that moment, it hit me—the reason behind my discomfort, the root of all my unease. I had been so consumed with the desire to please others, to fit in, that I had neglected to be true to myself. Guilt gnawed at me as I realized that I had put on a façade, pretending to share the same interests and passions as my new friends. The weight of my inauthenticity bore down on me, suffocating my spirit. I was doing the same thing again: putting on a mask and going along with others to fit in.

Taking a deep breath, I gathered my courage. The words trembled on my lips, but I knew they had to be spoken. "Naina, I need to be honest with you. I appreciate your invitation, but horror movies aren't really my thing. I apologize if I gave you the wrong impression at the party. I was simply nervous about making new friends."

Naina's expression softened, and a gentle smile graced her lips. "Oh, Esha, there's no need to apologize. We all have different interests, and that's what makes us unique. I had a feeling that horror might not align with your preferences, especially considering your love for cutesy décor. It's completely okay!"

A wave of relief washed over me, and gratitude swelled within my chest. "Thank you for understanding. I genuinely want to befriend you but don't want to pretend to enjoy something that doesn't resonate with me."

Naina nodded with a genuine and reassuring smile. "Friendship shouldn't be built on pretense or the need to conform. Let's explore activities that genuinely align with our interests. How about planning a spa day or going to that bridal show we talked about together?"

My heart felt lighter, and a genuine smile spread across my face. "That sounds amazing, Naina. Let's plan something delightful that truly reflects both our passions."

With a newfound sense of authenticity, I recited the acceptance mantra once again, this time with genuine intent. I acknowledged my feelings, mistakes, and the transformative journey I had undertaken to rectify them. At that moment, a semblance of peace enveloped me, a quiet acceptance of who I was and a resolve to live authentically.

Taking a deep breath, I lingered in the bathroom, repeatedly splashing water on my face. The cool droplets washed away the remnants of unease, carrying them down the drain. As I emerged, a renewed sense of calm and clarity embraced me, replacing the turmoil that consumed my being. With a tranquil heart, I faced the tasks before me, ready to embrace the day with unwavering authenticity and a genuine acceptance of myself and others.

28

Embracing the Ever-Evolving Path

That evening, after a long day at work, I made my way to Nandini's house, eager to share the revelations of the day. The weight of my newfound knowledge pressed upon me, urging me to confide in a friend who understood. The sun had begun its descent, casting a warm golden glow over the streets as I approached Nandini's front door. I took a deep breath and rang the doorbell, anticipation coursing through my veins.

Nandini greeted me with a warm smile, her eyes gleaming with curiosity. "Esha, you seem like you have something important to share. Come in, tell me everything," she said, gesturing for me to enter.

With a heavy heart, I recounted everything that had happened during the party and my subsequent reflections. "Nandini, I must admit, I fell into the same trap as before. I was being fake, pretending to be someone I'm not, just to make new friends. It's a mistake I made in the past, and it ruined me. I thought I had learned from it, but I can't believe I did it again."

Nandini listened attentively, her eyes filled with empathy. She led me to the cozy living room, and we settled on the comfortable couch surrounded by soft cushions. "Esha, self-discovery is a journey that can take a lifetime," she said, her voice gentle yet firm. "We're constantly evolving, learning new lessons about ourselves and the world. It's okay to stumble and make mistakes. What truly matters is how we use those experiences to grow and shape our character."

I nodded, the weight on my shoulders lightening with her words. "I guess you're right, Nandini. This is just another chapter in my ongoing story of self-improvement. I managed to recognize my mistake and work through it. Life is full of lessons, and no matter how much we think we know, there will always be more to learn."

Her eyes sparkled with understanding. "Exactly, Esha. It can be both frightening and liberating to accept that we'll never have all the answers. But it's in embracing that uncertainty that we truly grow. Every day, I learn new things about myself, and I grow and change, as do you."

Her wisdom washed over me, comforting me like a warm embrace. I realized that this journey of self-discovery was not about reaching a final destination but rather about the continuous process of learning and evolving. I had taken a step forward by calmly assessing the situation, engaging in self-talk and introspection, and rectifying my mistake. It was a valuable lesson learned, and I was determined to use it to become a better version of myself.

Over the next few months, I embraced several small lifestyle changes. The first significant change was establishing a consistent sleep schedule, which proved challenging initially but gradually became a habit. Mornings began with a refreshing concoction of honey and lemon water, infusing me with vitality and setting a positive tone for the day. I embarked on extended walks and jogs, immersing myself in the beauty of nature and allowing my thoughts to wander freely.

Taking charge of my meals became a delightful adventure. Nandini and I would gather every weekend, armed with recipes for nutritious and delicious dishes. We explored fat-free recipes online, experimenting with flavors and ingredients, savoring the joy of culinary creativity. Our dinner gatherings became cherished moments of camaraderie and nourishment for both body and soul.

My finances had improved over the months. I diligently followed Nandini's advice, cutting back on unnecessary expenses in groceries, malls, dining out, transportation, and beauty treatments. I embraced homemade alternatives and found joy in taking care of myself without relying on expensive services. The newfound discipline paid off, and I watched my savings grow steadily.

With the savings I had accumulated, I felt a weight lifted off my shoulders as I successfully settled two of my debts. The sense of relief and joy was overwhelming. I realized the power of understanding and managing money wisely. It was a transformative journey that taught me the importance of restraint, self-discipline, and embracing a new mindset.

With each passing day, I felt a surge of energy within me. My weight began to melt away, a physical manifestation of my inner transformation. The scale reflected my progress, shedding five kilograms in the first six weeks alone. It was a significant achievement that brought me immense happiness and Nandini's unwavering support.

With determination and persistence, these changes became ingrained in my daily life. The once-difficult routines now felt effortless, and even Reema joined me on occasional morning walks, appreciating the serenity of the early hours. We bonded over experimenting with recipes on holidays, relishing the joy of newfound health and happiness. Our shared experiences deepened our friendship, creating a bond forged through mutual growth and support.

Beyond the physical changes, I noticed a remarkable transformation taking place within myself. I found myself becoming calmer and more patient in difficult situations, taking a moment to reflect on my options before deciding. The acceptance mantra became my guiding light, helping me to embrace the present moment and learn from every experience.

To aid in this journey of self-discovery, I started keeping a diary. Its pages became a sacred sanctuary where I poured my thoughts and emotions onto the blank canvas. Writing allowed me to untangle the complexities of my inner world, gaining clarity and perspective. I found solace in the written word, a companion on this path of self-reflection.

And now, as I packed my bags for my much-awaited vacation back home, I couldn't help but feel a sense of contentment. I was in a good place in my life, surrounded by genuine friendships and armed with the knowledge that I was continually evolving. The anticipation of surprising Ayushi on her upcoming birthday filled me with excitement and joy. Life was full of surprises, and I was ready to embrace them with open arms.

With this newfound acceptance in my heart, I boarded the train that would take me back to Bhoojpur. The rhythmic motion of the train lulled me into a state of tranquility as I gazed out at the passing landscapes. The once-familiar sights of the bustling cityscape of Mumbai gradually faded into the distance, replaced by the laid-back serenity of Bhoojpur.

29

Choosing the Path Less Comfortable

After a seeming endless wait, changing to a connecting train at Varanasi and a bus at Chandauli, I finally disembarked, greeted by the familiar sights and sounds of Bhoojpur. The lush green landscape with quaint streets stretched out before me, adorned with colorful houses and vibrant flowers that added a touch of serenity to the atmosphere. The gentle rustling of leaves and the distant sound of the flowing stream created a soothing symphony that echoed in my ears.

As I strolled through the streets, memories from my childhood flooded my mind, intertwining with the present moment. I couldn't help but be captivated by the profound sense of homecoming that enveloped me. The warmth of familiarity wrapped around my heart, pulling me closer to the place where I truly belonged.

Approaching my childhood home, a mixture of anticipation and worry stirred within me. What awaited me behind those doors? Would my loved ones still recognize the person I had become? The moment of truth arrived as I stepped onto the porch, and there they were—my parents, their faces lighting up with pure joy, their eyes filled with unspoken love and pride.

Tears of happiness welled up in my eyes as my mother enveloped me in a tender embrace. "We've missed you more than words can express, my dear," she whispered, her voice filled with emotions that mirrored my own.

Overwhelmed by a surge of emotions, my voice trembled as I replied, "I missed you all so much. It feels like I've come back to where I truly belong."

My father, wearing a warm smile, approached us. "You've grown into such a remarkable person, my child. We are immensely proud of you," he said, his voice filled with paternal affection and admiration.

The walls of our home echoed with laughter and tears as we made our way inside. Surprising Ayushi, who had been unaware of my arrival, rushed into my arms, her tears mingling with mine as we shared a profound moment of reunion. The house embraced me like an old friend, its familiarity providing solace and grounding me in the present moment.

Days slipped by in a gentle rhythm, allowing me to rediscover the simplicity and beauty of a humble life. The early morning breeze caressed my cheeks as I woke up to the melodious chirping of birds. The scent of the water greeted me at every turn, filling my senses with a sweet nostalgia that evoked childhood memories.

Reconnecting with my childhood friends became a priority. We spent hours reminiscing about our shared adventures, revisiting the secret hideouts we had created, and recounting the dreams we had woven together under the vast blue sky. In their presence, I found comfort and a reminder of the unbreakable bonds forged in the innocence of youth. I visited Nandini's parents and conveyed her warm regards and gifts.

However, amidst the joy and tranquility, moments of doubt and shadows cast their pall over me. The familiarity of the village contrasted sharply with the tumultuous experiences I had faced in Mumbai. The memories of the hardships I endured there weighed heavily on me, threatening to dampen the newfound peace I had discovered.

One evening, as the sun began its descent and painted the sky in hues of orange and pink, I found myself at my cherished stargazing spot—a quiet meadow that slowly started to get illuminated by the shimmering constellations above. The twinkling stars whispered secrets of the universe, urging me to embrace the endless possibilities that lay ahead. It had been so long since I last lay here, gazing up at the vast expanse of the night sky.

Memories of a particular night flooded back when I had sought solace in the stars that had always brought me comfort and clarity. But that night, they had abandoned me, obscured by clouds. It felt as if even my trusted companions had turned their backs on me. It was a lonely and disheartening experience that I couldn't easily forget. I paused and stared at the stars, searching for answers within their depths. Was it right to pursue my dreams in Mumbai? Had I been naive in my pursuit of a rushed future? The whispers of doubt grew louder, echoing in my mind, threatening to unravel the newfound clarity I had discovered. I closed my eyes, took a deep breath, and allowed the village air to fill my lungs. In this moment of stillness, I realized I couldn't run away from my inner turmoil, nor could I ignore the struggles that had shaped me.

A gentle breeze caressed my cheeks as if offering its support in my internal battle. Opening my eyes, I surveyed the village that had witnessed my growth and transformation. It had provided me with a temporary escape, a refuge from the chaos of the city. But the struggles I had faced in Mumbai had been an integral part of my journey—an arduous path that had molded me into the person I had become.

As I gazed at the familiar constellations, I couldn't help but giggle at my own silly thoughts. I stood up slowly, shouting to the stars, "I'm back, my old friends! I've made mistakes, hurt others and myself, but I've changed and grown. I've discovered things about myself that were once hidden. I hope you'll continue to watch over me and guide me on my journey!" With that, I waved goodbye to the stars, knowing I had only one more day in the village before returning to Mumbai. The village had rekindled a sense of peace and connection within me, yet I wondered if I could carry that with me into the bustling streets of the metropolis.

With newfound determination, I continued my journey of rediscovering my village, cherishing each interaction, each embrace, and each moment of contemplation.

As the time to bid farewell to the village drew near, standing on the outskirts of Bhoojpur, a serene smile graced my lips. The picturesque beauty of the village unfolded before me, illuminated by the golden rays of the rising sun. The bittersweet nostalgia tugged at my heartstrings, but within me burned a newfound determination and acceptance.

I looked back at the village, where I had rediscovered the essence of simplicity and community. It nurtured my spirit, reminding me of the values that had shaped me. But I couldn't let fear hold me back from continuing my journey. The challenges I faced in Mumbai were an essential part of my growth, and I was ready to confront them head-on.

With each step toward the departing train, I carried the essence of my village within me—the values, the sense of community, and the serenity that had shaped my character. Mumbai awaited me, a city of opportunities and challenges that would continue to test my resilience and push me to evolve. As the train pulled away, I bid farewell to the village that had nurtured my spirit, knowing that I would forever carry its essence within me wherever my journey led.

30

Navigating the Waves of Non-acceptance

It had been a couple of months since I returned to Mumbai, and the city was beginning to feel more like home. I had made a conscious decision to return, and now I was settling into my familiar surroundings with a sense of comfort. My friendship with Reema had grown stronger than ever, and I considered myself fortunate to have made friends with many colleagues, including my boss. Life seemed to be falling into place.

On a relaxed Sunday evening, as the sun started its descent, Reema and I sat together, having just finished a movie. However, there was an uneasiness about her that I couldn't ignore. Sensing her inner turmoil, I gently probed, encouraging her to share what was on her mind.

"Esha, I don't quite know how to say this," Reema began hesitantly, her voice tinged with a mix of excitement and nervousness.

"What is it?" I asked, my curiosity piqued.

She took a deep breath and continued, "Tomorrow, I have an interview at Impression."

I was taken aback. "At my company?" I exclaimed, surprised by the revelation.

Reema nodded, a glimmer of enthusiasm shining in her eyes. "Yes, your boss, Sanjay, whom I met at the dinner party we hosted, offered me a position. It's a fantastic opportunity to work as a Senior Designer for their wedding collection."

A wave of conflicting emotions washed over me. Though I might have provided appropriate responses on the surface, I was a tumultuous mess inside. Excusing myself, I left the room, finding myself on the rooftop, where I had been frequenting more often. The appetite for dinner vanished amidst the chaos brewing within me.

Thoughts raced through my mind like a whirlwind. "Oh no, not again! Why do things go wrong when everything seems to be going right?" I agonized silently. Reema was my dear friend; I should have been happy for her. But deep down, I felt a mixture of insecurity and fear. What if our working relationship broke down once more? I dreaded the possibility of arguments and disputes, just like in the past when our personal and professional lives intertwined.

Reema was undeniably talented and hardworking, and I couldn't help but wonder if she would soon become everyone's favorite in the office. In contrast, my standing in the workplace was still relatively fragile—I was a newbie. At some point, we might even end up rivals as we try to make our way up the corporate ladder. The unease and jealousy crept into my thoughts. "What if they like her more than me? Will I become overshadowed?" I questioned myself, grappling with the complexities of my own emotions.

I scolded myself internally, attempting to silence the storm raging within. But my mind refused to cooperate, swinging from self-loathing to resentment towards Reema. I was enveloped in a sea of shame and insecurity, perplexed by the difficulty of accepting her success with grace and genuine happiness.

Finally, after what felt like an eternity, I managed to break free from the whirlpool of my thoughts. Realizing that I needed someone to confide in, I immediately texted Nandini. She was engaged in a social engagement, but understanding the urgency of my message, she promised to meet me early the following day at a nearby park.

As the morning sun rose, I anxiously met Nandini at the park, pouring out the entire story, every detail Reema had shared with me. Nandini listened attentively, her understanding gaze offering solace and support amidst the chaos of my mind.

"Reema joining your workplace is a reality that you must accept," Nandini said, her voice filled with understanding.

"But Nandu, I've tried to come to terms with it. I really have," I replied, my disappointment evident. Anger towards myself welled up inside me.

"Calm down, Eshu. Your thoughts have been consuming you unconsciously. They're negatively affecting your mind. Please, just take a moment to breathe and find your calm," Nandini soothingly urged me.

"I'm sorry. I just can't accept this. The acceptance mantra doesn't seem to work in this situation," I confessed, my frustration lingering.

"That's alright. There are times when acceptance feels impossible. Let's try to find a way to navigate through this. Remember, the first step is accepting the non-acceptance. And it's okay to let your emotions flow," Nandini reassured me.

"Let them flow? As I mentioned earlier, I'm unable to accept this situation. I've been trying to accept my non-acceptance since yesterday, but it's just not working. I don't understand," I muttered irritably.

We strolled through the park, eventually finding a peaceful spot beneath a sprawling tree. Nandini resumed speaking, "When the habit of acceptance takes root within you, you'll no longer fight against others. Instead, you'll accept each person as they are. This not only dissipates the river of sorrow but also eradicates negative emotions like jealousy, attachment, comparison, and greed that sprout within it. If, even after all this, you're still unable to accept the situation, the best course of action is to accept your non-acceptance. Then, ask yourself, 'Can I now accept the situation?' Keep repeating this question until you can genuinely accept the situation and your emotions."

I mulled over her words, attempting to digest them. "Emotions can be so difficult to manage! I am trying to understand what emotions really are," I suggested.

Nandini nodded in agreement. "Indeed, emotions stem from our subconscious mind, which automatically generates responses to certain stimuli. From childhood, we develop fixed responses to external triggers stored within our subconscious. For example, we instinctively pull our hands away from fire without conscious thought. That's the automatic response programmed into our subconscious mind."

She continued, "Likewise, certain fixed responses are triggered within different parts of our bodies when the subconscious mind interprets and matches an input to a stored response. When we feel cornered or threatened, depending on our childhood programming, our subconscious may evoke emotions like fear or anger. Suppressing negative emotions can have destructive consequences."

"Destructive effects?" I inquired, perplexed by her statement.

"Yes," Nandini confirmed. "Many individuals allow negative emotions—hatred, sorrow, depression, restlessness, distrust, bitterness, anger, fear, worry, envy, stress, resistance, and revenge—to dwell within them. These emotions have a detrimental impact on both mental and physical health. It wouldn't be far-fetched to say that our mind holds the reins of our well-being. A heart attack can be seen as a 'hate attack' or a 'thought attack' caused by intense negative feelings."

"Really?" I questioned, finding it difficult to believe.

Nandini nodded earnestly. "A mind consumed by anxiety can lead to psychosis. Anxiety spreads like poison throughout the body, creating a breeding ground for disease. Negative emotions drain the enthusiasm from the mind, causing depression. Individuals battling prolonged depression often lose their will to live. Recovery from illness can be a long, arduous journey for such individuals."

"On the other hand, those who embrace life with eagerness and enthusiasm tend to recover quickly. They can triumph over even the most fatal of diseases. Anger and stress create tension in our nerves, leading to pain that can persist for hours or even days," she explained.

"Days?" I raised my eyebrows in disbelief.

"Sounds unbelievable, but it's true," Nandini affirmed. "Some individuals prone to anger and stress may even require sleeping pills to find solace."

Feeling overwhelmed, I asked, "What's the solution?"

Nandini looked at me with a serene smile, ready to unveil the solution that had been simmering within her. It was an answer I had an inkling of, but hearing it spoken aloud by her felt like a revelation.

"The solution is acceptance," she said, her voice carrying a profound weight. "Acceptance and cultivating positive emotions can rapidly reduce nerve tension. Imagine a lion preparing to attack its prey. Before pouncing, the lion looks into the prey's eyes. If it senses fear, it strikes immediately. But if the prey displays no fear, the lion waits patiently until the prey loses confidence. And if the prey remains fearless, even after a considerable time, the lion chooses a different path."

"Wow, is that really true?" I asked, awe evident in my voice.

Nandini nodded. "Yes, it is. The same principle applies to disease and health. In the example with the lion, the lion represents disease. It preys upon those who are filled with fear and negative emotions. However, it veers away when it encounters emotions like love, joy, peace, compassion, faith, goodwill, purity, and abundance. Each and every emotion within us seeks to be understood."

"It's as if emotions themselves are living beings needing understanding," I mused.

"They do need that understanding," Nandini affirmed. "Whenever an emotion arises, it's akin to that emotion saying, 'Please understand me.' Every emotion emerges, seeking release and liberation. But due to the subconscious programming we have undergone since childhood, we fail to truly understand the emotion. Instead, we react to it immediately, without rational thought, in an attempt to escape from it. What we should do, however, is learn to witness and understand what the emotion truly represents."

Curiosity piqued, I asked, "And what is the true nature of an emotion?"

"An emotion is like a child yearning to be understood by its parents," Nandini explained. "The child may throw a tantrum to grab attention. Yet, if the parents are unaware of the deeper needs hidden behind the tantrum, they may silence the child through scolding or distractions. Similarly, we often suppress or divert our emotions. But these methods do not genuinely help in releasing the emotion."

"How, then, do we release our emotions?" I asked, eager to uncover the solution.

"By opening up and sharing your feelings with a trusted friend, relative, or counselor," Nandini suggested. "Sharing your negative emotions with someone you trust can bring about a sense of lightness and relaxation. Sometimes, merely talking about your feelings can set many of them free. The person you confide in can also offer attentive listening and valuable advice."

"Like the way I opened up to you," I reflected, realizing the significance of our conversation.

"Yes, exactly," Nandini replied, a warm smile gracing her face. "That's one of the most common and effective methods. Additionally, you can engage your intellect and confront your emotions. For instance, if the feeling of fear is troubling you, take it as a challenge and overturn it. If you constantly worry about potential illnesses, face this feeling head-on by asking yourself probing questions that lead you to the bare facts."

"What kind of questions?" I inquired, eager to learn more.

"For example," Nandini began, "reflect on the past instances when you were worried about various illnesses. Did all of them happen to you? No, only a few did. Were they as severe or dangerous as you feared? Perhaps only one or two were. And were you able to overcome those instances? Yes, you were. This realization indicates that you have the strength to face any future challenges, should they arise. It signifies that your body is healthy and growing stronger every day, aided by your positive self-talk."

I absorbed her words, contemplating their significance. "So, by employing the power of logic, I can invalidate my emotions?"

Nandini nodded. "Precisely. In the same vein, when confronted with situations that evoke negative emotions such as sorrow, disappointment, anger, or despair, remind yourself that you are joy traveling through the tunnel of despair, or peace navigating through the tunnel of anger, or bright faith journeying through the tunnel of despair."

I felt a glimmer of hope ignited within me. "So, this negative feeling I'm experiencing right now is merely a temporary occurrence, and soon, I'll emerge from this tunnel of negativity into the brightness of love, joy, and peace?"

"Yes, exactly," Nandini confirmed, her voice resonating with reassurance. "It's crucial to internalize the temporary nature of these thoughts and emotions. They come and go, much like flares shooting across the sky. They appear for a time in the sky of our awareness, and then they fade away."

I sighed, a mix of relief and frustration. "But when those flares shoot, they can really consume you. The pain feels unbearable."

"I understand," Nandini empathized. "However, as we resist the emotions that arise, we inadvertently energize and strengthen them."

I pondered her words, realizing the truth they held. "Hmm..."

Sometimes our emotions are exaggerated by our mind. What may appear to be a heavyweight emotion of the order of 50 kilograms may turn out to be not even 5 grams. But this truth is revealed only through deep observation.

"Are you trying to say my emotions are exaggerated by my mind?" I asked, seeking clarification from Nandini.

"Yes, our mind tends to do that. But you have to introspect and observe the process to understand it," she replied, her voice filled with wisdom.

Nandini continued guiding me through the intricacies of handling emotions. "Whenever an incident happens, we often choose negative words to describe our feelings, like 'I am worried... I am feeling scared... I am depressed... I am very angry... I am so restless...' and so on. But when you label your feelings as 'worried,' for example, that label triggers further worry."

Hanging on to her every word, I absorbed her advice and nodded, eager to understand more.

"Hence, don't label the feelings arising in your body. Simply view the tension, muscle contractions, changed vibrations, etc., as they are, and tell yourself, 'Like every incident, this incident has come to teach me something by presenting me with a challenge.' The solution to this problem lies hidden within the problem itself. I need to discover it and use it as a ladder for progress. I will definitely reap the rewards of overcoming this challenge," Nandini explained, her voice resonating with conviction.

"Challenges are a doorway to growth. I have learned that the hard way," I admitted, reflecting on the lessons life had taught me.

"But it's been very useful, wouldn't you say?" Nandini smiled, acknowledging my journey.

"Definitely!" I agreed readily, feeling a sense of gratitude for the wisdom I had gained.

Nandini further illustrated her teachings with an analogy. "You can also determine the worth of each incident. For instance, suppose you go to a shop to buy a matchbox, and the shopkeeper is selling it for twice the market value. Will you buy it?"

"Of course not!" I responded immediately, understanding the scenario.

"Why?" Nandini questioned, encouraging me to delve deeper.

"Well, it's obvious, isn't it? I know that the shopkeeper is asking for more than its actual worth," I explained, the realization sinking in.

"Exactly! So, we must adopt the same approach to deal with life's incidents. If you find yourself upset over a trivial incident, you may be paying more attention to it than its worth. For example, getting angry at someone for speaking ill of you without validating the truth wastes mental energy and harms your health for a trivial reason," Nandini elaborated, emphasizing the importance of perspective.

As her teachings continued, I began to feel a sense of relief. My mind had cooled down, allowing me to think objectively. I understood that being a victim of jealousy in this manner was wrong.

"When you are happy, you become a relaxed magnet, attracting the best and the highest into your life," Nandini said, leading me toward a greater understanding.

"But how can I be happy?" I asked, still searching for answers.

"You can be happy by knowing the real reason for your happiness. Think of it this way: If Reema becomes a senior designer, what's the harm in it? You can progress too. In reality, whether you accept it or not, it will not change what happens, but by holding on to feelings of jealousy and envy, you are harming only yourself. A person who rejoices in others' success is more receptive to success. If you remain happy with Reema's success, you are harmonizing with success in your own life. With better harmony, success will come easily to you, too," Nandini explained, enlightening me with her wisdom.

"Yes, I do get it. I can see I am wrong. I should, in fact, be inspired by Reema. I should learn from her, shouldn't I?" I responded, feeling a shift in my perspective.

"Yes. You might as well think of it this way: instead of having any other colleague, you are getting your good friend as a colleague. Wouldn't that be nice?" Nandini suggested, helping me find a positive aspect to focus on.

"Actually, yes. I was so consumed with my own insecurity that I just couldn't think of that," I admitted, feeling a sense of relief.

"You just need to change your viewpoint a little bit, and a small change can turn a negative incident into a positive one. And just think, how would you feel if Reema thought the same way about you?" Nandini pointed out, urging me to consider the flip side.

The thought of Reema feeling the way I had, made me shudder, and I realized the importance of empathy and fairness.

"Yeah, exactly. You must have heard people saying, 'Treat others as you want yourself to be treated.' It means if you want to be respected by others, you must respect others. If you experience jealousy at the success of others, how do you expect others to celebrate your success? Would it feel good if you were at the zenith of success, and there was no one out there to share that joy with you?" Nandini questioned, prompting me to reflect on the consequences of my actions.

"No, I don't fancy that situation. What you are saying is correct. While dealing with others, I should stop and evaluate how I would feel if someone else treated me like this. This pondering does make it easy for me," I admitted, feeling a growing sense of acceptance.

Nandini smiled, pleased with my progress. "Yes, so are you good now?"

"Well, talking it out with you has helped me a lot; and I feel much lighter and relieved. I am going to work and get out of this tunnel soon. Thanks a ton!" I expressed my gratitude, feeling a renewed sense of determination.

"You're welcome! Is that all? Should we make a move? It's getting late!" Nandini suggested, reminding me of the passing time.

"Yes! For now, that's all," I replied, feeling a sense of closure to our conversation. I hugged Nandini tightly, grateful for her presence in my life and the guidance she had provided.

As expected, Reema cleared the interview and would join me at Impression in just a few weeks. Thinking objectively and accepting the incident helped me overcome my emotions and gain clarity. I realized that my initial insecurities had been exaggerated, and Reema's success was well-deserved. Since my turnaround, I had been working hard, focusing on my own goals without the need for envy or jealousy. With the knowledge imparted by Nandini, I had developed qualities like self-discipline, courage, power of discrimination, patience, a flexible intellect, and mental stability.

I began to experience wonder, love, joy, peace, and better health. I understood that my feelings not only affected my physical well-being but also influenced my efficiency, creativity, and productivity. With a lighter heart and a clearer mind, I was confident that my hard work and newfound perspective would lead me to where I wanted to go.

31

Back to the Future

Esha leaned back in her chair, a wide smile spreading across her face as she finished recounting her story. The miracle of her recovery never ceased to amaze her, no matter how much time had passed. Her life now was vastly different from what it had been before. She had come to accept Reema working with her, and all the initial awkwardness had faded away. In fact, Esha had discovered that working with Reema was not only enjoyable but also highly productive. They had developed an understanding of each other's styles and thinking processes, which made their work flow seamlessly. Reema had taken notice of the drastic changes and impressive results, often joining Esha in her busy schedule.

Anita, who had listened intently to Esha's story, wore a stunned expression on her face. "Wow, Esha! You truly had quite a roller coaster ride back then. But it was incredibly brave of you to face your situation head-on. It's one thing to receive advice, but it's a true challenge to actually follow it. Thank you so much for opening up to me. I've learned so much about life and how to deal with its challenges. You have no idea how much this means to me." Anita's eyes sparkled with excitement.

Esha smiled warmly at Anita's heartfelt response. "I'm glad this could help you. Actually, I've come to realize that these lessons can benefit anyone. You don't have to be in a dire situation to get your life on a better track. Internalizing these lessons and implementing these simple techniques even on ordinary days can further enhance your life!"

Anita nodded eagerly, absorbing Esha's words. "Yes, I noticed how Nandini helped you gradually take care of the different aspects of a balanced life. That's how I'll start, too – by accepting my current phase and seeking out the positives. Working on these facets will make me feel more in control of my life. What an empowering feeling that will be!" Anita closed her eyes and smiled, momentarily lost in a dream of her perfect future. Esha playfully nudged her, bringing her back to the present. "Wake up and get to work then! Just dreaming about it won't get you there."

Anita's expression turned thoughtful as she voiced another concern. "Actually, that's another thing I wanted to ask you. How were you able to stick to your decisions? I mean, I've made certain small decisions in the past, and I do follow through for a few days. But then procrastination takes over. Some things, like designing something new or experimenting with materials, come naturally to me and don't require that extra push. But when it comes to things like jogging or going to the gym, it all feels so monotonous and easy to avoid!"

Esha chuckled, recognizing the familiar struggle. "That's the hallmark of these things!" she replied. "Healthy food is often not as tasty, and good habits can be challenging to adopt. What kept me going was probably my past experiences and my purpose. I wasn't happy with my former self, and the burning desire to set things right again fueled my determination. Of course, there were times when I felt like giving up and reverting to my old ways, but I reminded myself of the desired outcome. Sometimes, I would put up small reminders around the house or ask Nandini to nudge me forward. I understand not everyone might feel the same urgency I did due to my incredibly derailed situation, but consistency is the key. You'll gradually get used to it. Just keep your purpose in mind!"

Anita smiled, nodding in agreement. The idea that these simple techniques could help streamline her life in all aspects resonated deeply with her. She expressed her gratitude to Esha and, after some general conversation about work, bid her farewell and headed home. She left with a renewed sense of energy, hope, and determination. Finally, she was ready to piece together her scattered life. It was an incredibly fulfilling and optimistic feeling.

For Esha, this phase marked not just a happy ending to a troubled story but also a joyous beginning to an even more miraculous future. She saw the transformative power of her journey and the potential it held for others. With a contented sigh, she looked ahead, eager to embrace the possibilities that lay ahead.

32

The Enigma of Existence

Esha found herself back on the familiar rooftop, her sanctuary amidst the chaos of life. This elevated haven held the weight of countless memories, both cherished and agonizing. As she gazed up at the night sky, adorned with countless shimmering stars, she felt a deep sense of contentment. After enduring a tumultuous journey, her rollercoaster existence had finally found equilibrium, transforming into a tapestry of beauty and balance. Gratitude swelled within her heart, recognizing the invaluable presence of friends like Nandini, who had stood by her side.

Lost in introspection, Esha couldn't help but reflect on the intricate twists her life had taken. Once basking in the glow of success and joy, an unexpected dip had plunged her into an abyss she never fathomed. Depression was a concept she had merely heard of in passing, never anticipating its relentless grip on her own spirit. Yet, from her newfound neutral vantage point, she heeded Nandini's words, urging her to seek positivity amidst the storm. Slowly but steadily, she had learned to embrace the silver linings in every situation. The mere thought of her past now elicited a smile, for it had acted as a catalyst for growth and transformation. However, a lingering question had begun to torment her recently—why? Why was she chosen to endure this arduous journey while others found solace through simpler means?

As her thoughts raced, an echo of Nandini's wisdom resonated within her. Everything happened for a reason, she had said. Perhaps there was a hidden purpose buried within her trials. Esha acknowledged that she was not alone in her struggles; many faced immense challenges. Yet, she belonged to a fortunate few who had risen above their tribulations, aided by Nandini's understanding and their unbreakable childhood bond. Not everyone possessed such empathetic souls in their lives, for it was difficult to comprehend something one had never experienced. However, Esha possessed an innate ability to grasp the depths of others' pain, particularly Anita's, and extended a compassionate hand. Their stories intertwined like threads of fate, allowing for shared understanding and growth.

In a moment of epiphany, it struck Esha like a bolt of lightning. Perhaps her experiences were not solely her burden to bear. Instead, they served as a bridge between her and those seeking solace. This newfound insight ignited a spark of excitement within her. Yet, a missing piece still eluded her; this revelation felt incomplete. Life, she knew, was brimming with miracles waiting to unfold. How did these miracles come to pass? Curious to delve deeper into the enigma, Esha resolved to bombard Nandini with her inquiries, eager to uncover the mysteries that lay ahead.

A few days had passed since their last meeting, and once again, they gathered at Dream Bean Café. After placing their lunch orders, they settled in for a heartfelt conversation.

"Nandu, I can't thank you enough for being my guiding light. My life has profoundly transformed, and I've been contemplating something lately. I believe it may be the impersonal purpose of my existence!" Esha's excitement radiated as she shared her newfound revelations and sought further guidance.

"Nandu, is it possible for a mere shift in thoughts to bring about such intense transformation? It almost feels like a fairy tale, how my perspective on things has shifted. Take Reema's promotion to Senior Designer, for example. Initially, it bothered me, but now I find solace in the same event."

"Eshu, it all stems from the mind. Allow me to illustrate with an example: Imagine a person preparing to sleep who unknowingly shifts their pillow and, at that moment, is struck with terror upon spotting a snake beneath it. Panic ensues, but when the person finally turns on the lights, they realize it was nothing but a harmless string. They discard the string and laugh at their own fear, subsequently drifting off to sleep without any worries.

"Now, consider the emotional state of that person when they believed a snake lurked beneath their pillow. Once they discovered it was merely a string, they felt a sense of security. This demonstrates how changing one's thoughts about a situation resolves the problem," Nandini explained.

Esha pondered Nandini's words, her mind delving into deeper realms. "So, you're saying these are tricks played by the mind?"

"Indeed. Have you ever wondered how sorrow infiltrates our lives? In truth, sorrow doesn't reside within specific incidents. Rather, it stems from the thoughts we harbor during or after those incidents. Our mind is the true source of our worries," Nandini elaborated.

"The same incident that brings sadness to some may bring joy to others. For instance, rain may be a blessing for a farmer but a source of annoyance for someone navigating the city. If sorrow were inherent in the incident itself, it would impact everyone equally. Instead, our mind labels, judges, and compares, thus creating happiness or sorrow," Nandini continued.

"So, can we say that the sorrows stem from the stories our mind creates after perceiving an incident?" Esha sought clarification.

"Exactly. The moment a person shifts their thoughts, everything changes. The very thing that once caused sorrow can become a source of happiness," Nandini affirmed.

Listening to Nandini's wisdom stirred even deeper contemplation within Esha's mind. "Nandu, I have another question."

"I've been contemplating this question for days, and I genuinely believe that your guidance has transformed my life. However, doubts still linger in my mind. What is the ultimate purpose of my life? Can this purpose be impersonal as well? Moreover, something strange happened to me recently. This might sound a bit stupid. While reciting my regular affirmations, such as 'My body is returning to its optimal shape and strength,' I felt a peculiar disconnect when I said, 'MY body.' Does that imply that 'my body' and 'me' are separate entities? Who am I then? I haven't arrived at any conclusions."

Esha continued, her inquiries pouring forth. "Could it be that 'me' is distinct from my body? Are my mind, intellect, and other aspects also detached from me? We often say, 'My mind isn't working,' 'A thought crossed my mind,' or 'I'm using my wit.' Does this imply that the 'I' in these sentences differs from the mind? Who is this 'I' that drives the mind and body? What is the purpose behind all of this?"

"Hold on, just hold on for a moment! So many questions all at once," Nandini chuckled, amusement dancing in her eyes.

"What can I do? The questions have been swirling within me, and I couldn't contain them any longer. That's why I had to ask you," Esha confessed.

"It's wonderful that you've brought forth these questions. Far from being stupid, these are the most profound questions that we can ever ponder. Your contemplation is leading you toward the true purpose, the ultimate goal of life. The spiritual realm of life encompasses this ultimate purpose," Nandini revealed.

"What are you saying?" Esha's curiosity brimmed, craving to uncover the profound truths that lay ahead.

"Picture this," she started, her words flowing like a gentle stream. "Imagine someone saying, 'My hand was wounded when I had been to the kitchen. I was scared when I found that it was bleeding profusely. I then thought of visiting the doctor to dress up the wound.' It's fascinating how the word 'I' is being used in different ways."

Esha furrowed her brow, her confusion evident. Nandini continued, determined to shed light on the matter. "When you say, 'I had been to the kitchen,' the 'I' refers to the body. It's as if you're considering yourself as the physical vessel. But then, when you say, 'My hand was wounded,' whom does 'My' truly refer to? If you still identified yourself with the body, you would have said, 'I was wounded.'"

Esha's eyes widened as the realization began to dawn on her. Nandini's voice carried a soft certainty as she continued, "You see, when you say, 'My hand was wounded,' you acknowledge yourself as the owner of the body. It's only when you detach yourself from the body that you can claim ownership, saying, 'My hand.' So, the point of reference for the 'I' has shifted from the body to the owner of the body within the same sentence."

Nandini's words held a captivating rhythm as she delved deeper into the subject. "And then, when you say, 'I was scared,' the 'I' refers to the mind. The mind has its own spectrum of emotions, ranging from fear to sadness, elation to despair. It is the realm where thoughts and feelings dance their intricate choreography. And when you say, 'I thought of visiting the doctor,' the reference shifts once again, this time to the intellect. Here, you assume yourself to be the intellectual faculties."

Esha listened intently, her mind grappling with the layers of understanding Nandini was unveiling. Her voice was filled with curiosity as she posed the question that had been nagging at her. "But if the point of reference keeps changing, if there are so many 'I's, then who am I, truly?"

Nandini's smile was like a gentle sunrise, casting warmth and clarity. "You are what remains," she replied softly. "Asking yourself 'Who am I?' is a powerful means of breaking free from the identification with the false 'I's. It's an invitation to delve into the depths of your being, to discover your true nature, your true self. Relentlessly questioning 'Who am I?' inevitably leads to the experience of your true being—the essence of who you are."

Esha's eyes shimmered with a blend of wonder and skepticism. This was all so new to her, like an unexplored realm of possibilities unfolding before her very eyes. "Really?" she murmured, her voice barely audible.

Nandini nodded, her gaze steady. "Indeed," she affirmed. "Consider this: What enables your eyes to see? What is the light that illuminates not only light itself but also darkness? Some call it Consciousness, God, the Source, or the Self. It is the life principle that breathes through every living being, permeating everything that exists. It is the very reason we are alive."

She paused for a moment, allowing the weight of her words to sink in. Then, she continued, her voice carrying a resolute conviction. "You are that 'Self' or 'Consciousness' that has become entangled in the illusion of identifying with the body and mind. But the truth is, you are neither the body, nor the mind, nor the intellect. Your true nature transcends these temporary veils."

Esha was momentarily speechless, her mind swirling with the profound implications of Nandini's teachings. Sensing her friend's struggle, Nandini pressed on, her voice soothing yet firm. "You just need to re-remember who you truly are," she said. "That is the ultimate aim of life—to know your true self and to establish yourself in the experience of that truth."

Nandini's words hung in the air, enveloping Esha in a cocoon of contemplation. She tried to assimilate the enormity of what had been shared with her. A question rose within her, and she found her voice again. "But if I am consciousness, the true self, and not this body, or this mind, then why is there so much sorrow and depression in the world? Why is there misery?"

Nandini's gaze softened. "Many people ponder the purpose of this world," she began, her voice resonating with empathy. "Some even question the very essence of existence, complaining about life itself. But they fail to see the subtle thread that weaves everything together."

Esha listened with rapt attention, captivated by Nandini's words. "If the creator had never brought this phenomenal world into existence, how would we ever know the nature of creation?" Nandini mused. "We wonder why some people are deceitful while others are noble, why some sing melodiously and others harshly, why some appear beautiful and others ugly. The missing link lies in understanding that without creation itself, without this vast tapestry of diversity, there would be no basis for comparison or understanding."

Esha's eyes widened as a flicker of understanding sparked within her. Nandini continued, her voice gentle yet resolute. "Just as a painter mixes colors to create new shades, even including black, so does the Creator bring forth a multitude of experiences. Black, although it may appear dark and somber, serves a vital purpose in the artist's palette. It adds depth and dimension, highlighting the beauty of other colors through contrast."

A smile graced Nandini's lips as she imparted her wisdom. "Deceit, too, plays its part in elevating the value of goodness. Distrust elevates the value of faith. Hatred uplifts the place for love in the scheme of life. Everything that exists has its importance, its place in the grand tapestry of creation. But when we view everything through our limited perception and indulge in preferences and judgments, we fail to grasp the higher perspective of life."

Esha nodded, a newfound clarity shining in her eyes. "So, we need to understand the grand game being enacted in the universe. We must grasp our role in the grand scheme of things," she said, her voice resolute. "If we continue to complain and dwell solely on the things around us, we miss the true essence of life."

Nandini's eyes gleamed with approval, her voice conveying the profound truth. "Exactly," she affirmed. "We need to shift our perspective and think from the creator's point of view. We must contemplate the creative intention behind this intricate dance of existence. And we will discover that the ultimate purpose of creation is the experience and expression of the highest creative potential."

Esha's mind brimmed with questions, and she voiced one that lingered in her thoughts. "But what about thoughts? Why do they cause so many problems through labeling and comparison?"

"Imagine yourself seated in a vast expanse of empty space, stretching infinitely in all directions. Could you fathom that this emptiness is the pinnacle of creation, the purest form of existence? And if someone told you that this boundless expanse is who you truly are, would it make any sense? Our human intellect and imagination would fall short of comprehending such a truth.

"However, let's suppose that within this limitless expanse, four walls suddenly manifest around you, and you are informed that this enclosed space is your home. Would you then be able to accept it? In principle, yes. Introducing these walls creates a sense of 'createdness' that lets you perceive the vast expanse. Without these walls, the empty space lacked meaning. Although you still occupy the same space as before, the walls serve the purpose of awakening your awareness to the expanse surrounding you."

"In essence, thoughts, irrespective of their content, can be likened to those walls," Esha interjected, connecting the dots of Nandini's teachings.

Nandini smiled, acknowledging Esha's understanding, and continued, "Thoughts serve the purpose of experiencing the silence that exists as a backdrop. If thoughts fulfill this role, they represent the highest form of creation. The experience of the unknowable, the transcendent, is the ultimate goal of life."

Esha marveled at the unfathomable nature of it all. "The purpose of life is so exquisitely beautiful. We get entangled in the stories our minds create, believing our thoughts to be true, which only aggravates our suffering. I wonder what would happen if people realized the true purpose behind their existence and the grand design of creation. The world would transform into something entirely different. Each individual would operate on a whole new level."

Nandini nodded in agreement. "Indeed, that's just the beginning. It's merely the tip of the iceberg. There is so much more to discover, but the experience surpasses the limitations of words," she added, evoking a sense of mystery.

After taking a moment to absorb it all, they decided to continue their conversation at a later time, recognizing the depth and significance of the topic they were exploring. With heartfelt goodbyes, they parted ways, eager to delve further into the realms of understanding.

33

The Divine Play

Soon, Esha found herself in the cozy confines of Nandini's house on a tranquil Sunday afternoon. Anand and Khushi had ventured out to watch a movie, leaving the space exclusively for Esha and Nandini.

Overwhelmed by the newfound wisdom that had dawned from their earlier conversation, Esha couldn't help but exclaim, "Oh my God, Nandu! You have ignited a deluge of questions within me. I'm gaining an entirely different perspective on the design and purpose of life."

Nandini smiled, "Well, the mission of our life on Earth is to fulfill the SOUL purpose. It is to cultivate a mind that is Steadfast, Obedient, Untainted, and Loving. Such a mind aids in realizing the experience of the true self and understanding the true cause of suffering, which lies in the illusion of being a separate individual."

"Could you elaborate on that?" Esha asked, eager to delve deeper.

"Certainly. All the people on Earth can be classified into five categories, represented by the fingers of our hand," Nandini elucidated. "The little finger exemplifies those who tirelessly work throughout the day, be they factory workers or homemakers. They have the ability to transform their workplace into a haven and bring solace to those around them."

Curiosity sparked in Esha's eyes as she inquired, "And what about the thumb?"

"The thumb symbolizes people in positions of power. How they wield their power depends on the purity and sacredness of their mind," Nandini answered. "The ring finger represents those who are perpetually restless, their minds flitting about like buttons on a remote control."

Esha's attention turned to the remaining fingers. "And what do the middle and index fingers signify?"

"The middle finger, the longest one, represents those who achieve greatness and reach lofty heights. The index finger, on the other hand, symbolizes a simpler, easygoing, and straightforward life, always pointing towards things of significance," Nandini explained.

Nandini continued, painting a vivid analogy, "Now, let's envision that God, the orchestrator of all suffering and joy in human life, inserts His hand into a massive pot with a small opening. Each of the five fingers within the pot undergoes diverse experiences. One may feel the painful prick of thorns, while another senses the softness of cotton. Some fingers may get stained, while others encounter the tender touch of flowers."

Eager for understanding, Esha inquired, "What does this signify?"

"In truth, all the fingers accumulate a variety of experiences, both suffering and joy, within the pot. But who is the true experiencer? The one experiencing it all is outside the pot, while the fingers themselves are merely mediums, bringing those varied experiences to Him," Nandini explained.

Perplexed, Esha further questioned, "But why do we then feel sorrow and happiness?"

"In reality, it is God alone who experiences everything through these fingers. He resides outside this pot called the Universe. However, each finger assumes the suffering or joy, success or failure, to be its own. It starts taking ownership of these experiences, forgetting they were never meant for it. The finger never consults the One outside the pot," Nandini clarified.

"So, the finger forgets that these experiences are not its own, but rather God is experiencing them through its body. The day all the fingers, all the categories of human beings, grasp this secret, a new awareness will awaken within them. They will comprehend the true essence of the SOUL purpose," Nandini concluded.

This revelation struck Esha like a bolt of lightning, jolting her mind out of its usual patterns. To think that the body was merely a vessel, a conduit for God to experience the world, was both astounding and enlightening. It was a truth that had been hidden in plain sight, yet so few had truly grasped its significance. The simplicity and clarity of it all overwhelmed her, leaving her momentarily speechless.

Gathering her thoughts, Esha posed her burning question, seeking further clarification. "So, in order for God to experience through us, we need to be in touch with Him, right?"

Nandini's response was resolute and unwavering. "Absolutely! When we are in a state of happiness, we are in touch with God. But when we succumb to sadness and lose that connection, we drift away from Him. To remain in constant harmony with God, we must cultivate the art of finding happiness even in the midst of suffering. It may take time and effort, and we may stumble along the way, but through introspection and deep contemplation, we can establish an unbreakable connection with God. And when that connection is firm, happiness becomes our eternal companion. How can someone who is connected to God ever be unhappy?"

Esha marveled at this new perspective on joy and suffering. It was a paradigm shift that challenged her previous understanding. "So, if I understand correctly," she began, "suffering only arises when I perceive myself as separate from God. And in moments of happiness, I am simply a vessel for God's experiences. I am here to serve as a medium for Him."

Nandini's face beamed with delight as she saw the comprehension dawning in Esha's eyes. "Exactly! You've grasped it beautifully," she affirmed. "We are the messengers, the conduits through which God experiences the world and expresses His sublime qualities. The suffering we encounter is not personal but a part of the divine play. Once we internalize this truth, our perception of life is transformed, and our attachment to the outcomes of our experiences diminishes. We begin to embrace our role as faithful servants, and our connection with the divine deepens."

Esha felt a surge of elation and clarity. The pieces of the puzzle were falling into place, revealing a grander picture of existence. After being lost in deep reflection for a few moments, she further questioned, "It is so liberating to be able to see with such clarity. But still, I feel I have understood this intellectually. Wouldn't it be far more profound to get a first-hand experience of this divine play?"

Sensing that their exploration needed a practical exercise for experiencing the wisdom, Nandini gently guided Esha through a process of self-observation. "Let's do an exercise. First, close your eyes and focus your attention on one of your hands," she instructed. "Take a moment to observe and explore the sensations and feelings associated with it. Then, with your eyes closed, dive deeper and ask yourself, 'Am I this hand?' Pay close attention to the relationship you perceive between yourself and your hand."

In the silence that followed, Esha delved into a realm of introspection. She contemplated the question, allowing herself to delve into the depths of her being. Slowly, she began to realize that there were two distinct possibilities. Some might identify themselves as the hand, while others would feel a sense of detachment, recognizing that they were not the hand itself.

Nandini encouraged Esha to explore further. "If you feel that you are the hand, ask yourself, 'If this hand were to be severed, would I cease to exist? Would I perish?'" she urged.

Esha opened her eyes; her voice tinged with introspection. "No," she responded thoughtfully. "Even after imagining my hand being cut off, I still felt complete."

Nandini seized upon this realization, using it to deepen Esha's understanding. "Indeed," she affirmed. "Even if our limbs or body parts are lost, the essence of our being remains intact. The body may suffer injuries or endure hardships, but we, the true self, transcend these physical manifestations. We are eternal and unbounded. When we truly experience this truth, we begin to understand that our essence is separate from our physical form. We need to comprehend what we are not to discover what we truly are. This realization gradually dissolves our attachment to the body."

Esha closed her eyes once again, immersing herself in the process of self-inquiry. She explored each body part, negating her identification with them one by one. As she moved beyond the physical, she delved into the realm of thoughts, questioning their nature and origin. She realized that she was not the thoughts themselves. In the depths of her contemplation, she encountered an overwhelming silence—a profound stillness that resonated at the core of her being. Her body, she understood, was merely a vehicle for this stillness to experience itself.

Time seemed to slip away as Esha delved into this profound exploration. Fifteen minutes passed in what felt like an instant. It was then that Nandini gently interrupted the meditative state. "Open your eyes," she softly commanded.

Esha's face lit up with a radiant smile that emanated from the depths of her heart. "This experiment has revealed to me all that I am not," she exclaimed. "I will continue to delve into this inquiry whenever I find the time. But if we truly come to know ourselves, then what purpose does this body serve?"

Nandini responded, her voice filled with wisdom. "This body is simply a medium for our expression. Once we recognize our true nature, any occurrences within the body are no longer personal. We can view them as happenings to a dear friend accompanying us on this journey. While caring for and nurturing our bodies, we must remember that they are not our personal burden. We tend to the needs of our friend, administering care and healing when necessary. We enhance its capabilities and skills to serve us better in our self-expression. But we detach ourselves from personal identification with the body."

Esha pondered these words, seeking further clarification. "So, if I understand correctly, once I develop a detached perspective on my own life and the lives of others, will I truly comprehend that I am not this body?"

Nandini nodded in agreement. "Yes, precisely. When we detach ourselves from the identification with the body, we find ourselves observing the dramas of life with equanimity. Whether we receive criticism or praise, we are no longer affected in the same way. The ups and downs of the body become mere external events, and our happiness stems from the awareness of our own existence. It is a journey that requires practice and effort, but as you internalize this truth, you will find joy in the simple fact of being alive."

Esha pondered these words, struck by their profound simplicity. "People spend their lives searching for external reasons to be happy," she mused. "Yet, the true source of happiness lies within us. How many would truly acknowledge that their mere presence is the real cause of their own happiness?

"Thank you for opening my eyes to this opportunity to experience the true self," Esha expressed her gratitude to Nandini. "I am determined to continue with this experiment consistently."

Nandini smiled warmly, appreciating Esha's enthusiasm. "That's wonderful to hear! To further assist you, you can practice a powerful meditation that can help you access inner silence. Consider spending five minutes practicing it now."

Esha eagerly nodded, ready to embark on this new journey of self-discovery. She prepared herself to receive Nandini's guidance.

"Practice this meditation for a while, using a timer to keep track."

Esha felt a sense of readiness and determination. She set her phone's timer and settled into a comfortable position, ready to immerse herself in this practice.

"In this meditation," Nandini began, "as soon as a thought arises, you will give it a number, starting from 1. Wait for the next thought to arise, and then count 2."

Esha absorbed the instructions, understanding the essence of the practice. She started observing her thoughts and assigning them a numerical value, regardless of their content or nature.

Nandini continued, "Allow your thoughts to come and go naturally, without interference. Positive, negative, work-related, thoughts of confusion, or even thoughts of boredom—all of them should be counted. Even if you have thoughts about the meditation itself, simply give them a number and wait for the next thought.

"If you notice your mind wandering, gently bring your attention back to counting from 1."

"Continue observing and counting the thoughts as they arise and pass through your awareness." After the designated time had passed, Esha opened her eyes and met Nandini's gaze. "I completed the meditation. What's next?"

Nandini smiled, acknowledging Esha's dedication. "Now that you've practiced the meditation, I have three simple questions for you to consider. Reflect on your experience and answer truthfully: Was there a gap between thoughts? Were there moments when there were no thoughts? Were there moments when you were waiting for a thought?"

Esha took a moment to reflect on her meditation experience. "Yes," she replied thoughtfully. "I experienced gaps between thoughts, and there were moments when my mind seemed empty, devoid of any thoughts. I also noticed moments when I was eagerly waiting for the next thought to arise."

Nandini's eyes sparkled with excitement. "Excellent! Those moments of gap, emptiness, and anticipation are glimpses of something profound—the Source of everything. It is from this Source that thoughts arise."

Esha's curiosity grew. "So, those fleeting experiences were glimpses of the Source? I've had similar moments in the past when I felt a deep connection with nature. Are those related?"

Nandini nodded, her face radiating wisdom. "Absolutely. Those moments you've described when connecting with nature were indeed glimpses of the Source. It can manifest as a sense of stillness, oneness, or even a momentary absence of thoughts. They give us glimpses of the profound experience of the Source, the true self."

Esha's desire to understand and experience the Source intensified. "I want to delve deeper into this. I want to experience what you've experienced."

Nandini's eyes gleamed with reassurance. "And you will, my dear.

The key is to maintain consistency in your practice. Keep meditating, especially with the 'thought numbering' technique. With time and dedication, you will undoubtedly uncover profound experiences and insights."

Esha nodded eagerly, filled with determination and a newfound sense of purpose. She bid farewell to Nandini, leaving their session with a firm resolution to make the 'thought numbering' meditation a regular part of her daily routine.

Surprisingly, Esha found herself able to establish the habit quickly. Every morning, as she woke up, she diligently sat down for meditation, numbering her thoughts. Initially, it was challenging, as she would often lose count and then regain awareness, starting the count anew.

However, with each passing day, Esha noticed improvement. She became more proficient at maintaining the count and gradually increased both the count and the duration of her meditation. Within a span of two weeks, she had progressed to a point where she could comfortably sit for 15 minutes, deepening her practice.

Epilogue

Three weeks later, Esha and Nandini met for their usual lunch, continuing their journey of exploration. After ordering their meal, they engaged in their customary discussion, eager to share their progress and insights.

"I'm delighted to hear about your consistency in meditation," Nandini said with a smile. "You've made remarkable progress. You can now sit for longer stretches."

Esha beamed with pride. "Yes, it's been a gradual improvement. I'm able to sit with more ease and focus."

Nandini nodded approvingly. "That's excellent progress! Keep up the good work. Today, I want to share with you the concept of true success."

Esha's curiosity was piqued, "How is true success different from regular success?"

Nandini leaned forward, ready to impart her wisdom. "Regular success is often temporary and conditional. When life is going smoothly, we may feel content with our achievements. But when faced with difficulties and challenges, we start questioning whether our success truly brings lasting fulfillment."

Esha nodded in understanding. "So, you're saying that even though people strive for riches, power, and recognition, they might not find lasting fulfillment in those things?"

"Exactly," Nandini confirmed. "If you ask those who have achieved great success in their careers or amassed wealth, they will often admit that it hasn't brought them lasting fulfillment. There is a deeper purpose to human endeavor beyond these obvious goals."

She continued, "True success is an internal state of being. It is a state where we experience joy and completeness regardless of external circumstances. It is when our mind remains unshaken and peaceful in every situation."

Esha was intrigued. "So, true success is about realizing our true self and being established in that experience?"

Nandini nodded, a serene smile on her face. "Precisely. When we tap into the joy and completeness that come from being our true self, all other achievements pale in comparison. The joy we experience from external sources is temporary, like candle flames in the eternal sunlight of our true nature."

Esha pondered Nandini's words. "So, you're saying that the joy we experience from people and objects is merely a faint reflection of the bliss of our inner stillness?"

Nandini nodded once again. "Yes, it is the stillness of our mind that allows us to experience true joy. However, we often mistake the external sources of pleasure as the cause, and we become trapped in a cycle of chasing after desires, believing they will bring us happiness."

Esha's eyes widened. "That's a profound perspective. I never thought of it that way."

Nandini smiled, acknowledging Esha's realization. "It is indeed a different way of looking at things. True success is the ultimate purpose of all other successes we pursue in life. Through personal growth and development, we train our body and mind to serve the purpose of realizing and being established in our true nature."

She continued, explaining the hierarchy of needs and their role in human evolution. "There are various needs we fulfill on our path, from basic survival needs to love, belongingness, self-esteem, and the actualization of our potential. Yet, even after fulfilling these needs, we often sense a feeling of emptiness. This leads us to the ultimate need of realizing who we truly are—the source of life itself."

Esha listened attentively, captivated by Nandini's words. "So, just like mistaking a rope for a snake leads us to search for a stick to beat the illusion, mistaking worldly pursuits for true fulfillment can leave us searching for something that doesn't truly satisfy us?"

Nandini smiled, pleased with Esha's understanding. "Exactly. Wealth and other positive pursuits are not inherently wrong, but it is important to question whether they can truly bring us lasting peace and joy. We need to align our endeavors with our ultimate purpose while also achieving worldly success."

Esha's gratitude overflowed. "Nandu, I can't express how grateful I am for your guidance. My life was once unstable, and I was trapped in a vicious cycle. I even considered ending it all. But thanks to you, I'm discovering the ultimate purpose of life. You've helped me overcome my problems and find balance in all aspects of my life."

Nandini's eyes filled with warmth. "Eshu, it was my privilege to be a true friend to you. It was your sincerity and dedication to the techniques we discussed that truly helped you. I'm glad I could be there for you.

"I was merely a messenger, and all the wisdom and techniques that I've shared are from the retreat and follow-ups that I, too, have vastly benefitted from. I would urge you to participate in this retreat to gain a much more profound experience of this wisdom.

As they reminisced about their journey, Nandini and Esha shared a knowing smile. Their friendship had blossomed into a profound bond that facilitated their growth. Life had presented them with unexpected miracles, and each day brought new adventures. Together, they were moving closer to achieving the ultimate purpose of their balanced life, a beautiful life!

* * *

You can mail your opinion or feedback on this book to:
books.feedback@tejgyan.org

About Sirshree

Sirshree's spiritual quest, which began during his childhood, led him on a journey through various schools of philosophy and meditation practices. He studied a wide range of literature on mind science and spirituality. After a long period of deep contemplation on the truth of life, his quest culminated in attaining the ultimate truth.

Sirshree espouses, "All spiritual paths that lead to the truth begin differently but culminate at the same point – Understanding. This understanding is complete in itself. Listening to this understanding is enough to attain the Truth." Over the last two decades, he has dedicated his life to raise mass consciousness.

Sirshree has delivered more than 4000 discourses that throw light on this understanding. He has designed a system for wisdom, which makes it accessible to all. This system has inspired people from all walks of life to progress on their journey of the Truth. Thousands of seekers join in a virtual prayer for World Peace and Global Healing daily at 9:09 am and 9:09 pm.

About Tej Gyan Foundation

Tej Gyan Foundation is a non-profit organization founded on the teachings of Sirshree. The Foundation disseminates Tejgyan – the wisdom that guides one from self-development to Self-realization, leading towards Self-stabilization.

The Foundation's system for imparting wisdom has been assessed by international quality auditors and accredited with the ISO 9001:2015 certification. This wisdom has been presented in a simple, systematic, and practically applicable form that makes it accessible to people from all walks of life, regardless of religion, caste, social strata, country, or belief system.

The Foundation has centers in more than 400 cities and towns across India and other countries. The mission of Tej Gyan Foundation is to create a highly evolved society by leading seekers from negative thoughts to positive thoughts and further, from positive thoughts to Happy thoughts. A 'Happy thought' is the auspicious thought of being free from all thoughts, leading to the state of supreme bliss beyond thoughts.

If you seek such wisdom that leads you beyond mere knowledge, dissolves all problems, frees you from all limiting beliefs, reveals the true nature of divinity, and establishes you in the ultimate truth, then it is time to discover Tejgyan; it is time to rise above the mundane knowledge of words and experience Tejgyan!

The MahaAasmani Magic of Awakening Retreat

Self-development to Self-realization towards Self-stabilization

Do you wish to experience unconditional happiness that is not dependent on any reason? Happiness that is permanent and only increases with time? Do you wish to experience love, peace, self-belief, harmony in relationships, prosperity, and true contentment? Do you wish to progress in all facets of your life, viz. physical, mental, social, financial, and spiritual?

If you seek answers to these questions and are thirsty for the ultimate truth, then you are welcome to participate in the MahaAasmani Magic of Awakening retreat organized by Tej Gyan Foundation. This is the Foundation's flagship retreat based on the teachings of Sirshree.

The purpose of this retreat

The purpose of this retreat is that every human being should:

- Discover the answer to "Who am I" and "Why am I?" through direct experience and be established in ultimate bliss.
- Learn the art of living in the present, free from the burden of the past and the anxiety of the future.
- Acquire practical tools to help quieten the chattering mind and dissolve problems.
- Discover missing links in the practices of Meditation (*Dhyana*), Action (*Karma*), Wisdom (*Gyana*), and Devotion (*Bhakti*).

About Books by Sirshree

Sirshree's published work includes more than 150 book titles, some of which have been translated into more than 10 languages. His literature provides a profound reading on various topics of practical living and unravels the missing links in karma, wisdom, devotion, meditation, and consciousness.

His books have been published by leading publishing houses like Penguin, Hay House, Bloomsbury, Wisdom Tree, Jaico, etc. "The Source" book series, authored by Sirshree, has sold over 10 million copies. Various luminaries and celebrities like His Holiness the Dalai Lama, publishers Mr. Reid Tracy, Ms. Tami Simon and Yoga Master Dr. B. K. S. Iyengar have released Sirshree's books and lauded his work.

The Source
Attain Both, Inner Peace
and Worldly success

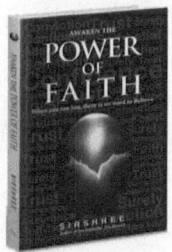

Awaken the Power of Faith
Discover the 7 Principles of the
Highest Power of the Universe

To order books authored by Sirshree, login to:

www.gethappythoughts.org

For further details, call: +91 9011013210

Tej Gyan Foundation – Contact details

Registered Office:
Happy Thoughts Building, Vikrant Complex, Near Tapovan Mandir, Pimpri, Pune 411017, INDIA. Contact: +91 20-27411240, +91 20-27412576

MaNaN Ashram:
Survey No. 43, Sanas Nagar, Nandoshi Gaon, Kirkatwadi Phata, Off Sinhagad Road, Taluka Haveli, Pune district - 411024, INDIA. Contact: +91 992100 8060.

WORLD PEACE PRAYER

Divine Light of Love, Bliss, and Peace is Showering;
The Golden Light of Higher Consciousness is Rising;
All negativity on Earth is Dissolving;
Everyone is in Peace and Blissfully Shining;
O God, Gratitude for Everything!

Members of Tej Gyan Foundation have been offering this impersonal mass prayer for many years. Those who are happy can offer this prayer. Those feeling low or suffering from illness can receive healing with this prayer.

If you are feeling troubled or sick, please sit to receive the healing effect of this prayer. Visualize that the divine white healing light is being showered on earth through the prayers of thousands and is also reaching you, bringing you peace and good health. You can dwell in this feeling for some time and then offer your gratitude to those offering the prayer.

A Humble Appeal

More than a million peace lovers pray for World Peace and Global Healing every morning and evening at 9:09. Also, a prayer (in Hindi) to elevate consciousness is webcast every day on YouTube at 3:30 pm and 9:00 pm IST. Please participate in this noble endeavor.

www.ingramcontent.com/pod-product-compliance
Lightning Source LLC
LaVergne TN
LVHW041921070526
838199LV00051BA/2696